Oliver Optic

**Fighting Joe: The fortunes of a staff officer**

A story of the great rebellion

Oliver Optic

**Fighting Joe: The fortunes of a staff officer**
*A story of the great rebellion*

ISBN/EAN: 9783337210878

Printed in Europe, USA, Canada, Australia, Japan

Cover: Foto ©ninafisch / pixelio.de

More available books at **www.hansebooks.com**

At the Battle of Antietam.
Page 143.

# FIGHTING JOE;

OR,

## THE FORTUNES OF A STAFF OFFICER.

### A Story of the Great Rebellion.

BY

## OLIVER OPTIC,

AUTHOR OF "THE SOLDIER BOY," "THE SAILOR BOY," "THE YOUNG LIEUTENANT,"
"THE YANKEE MIDDY," "RICH AND HUMBLE," "IN SCHOOL AND OUT,"
"WATCH AND WAIT," "WORK AND WIN," "THE RIVERDALE
STORY BOOKS," "THE BOAT CLUB," ETC.

---

BOSTON:
LEE AND SHEPARD, PUBLISHERS.
NEW YORK:
LEE, SHEPARD AND DILLINGHAM.
1873.

Entered according to Act of Congress, in the year 1865, by

WILLIAM T. ADAMS,

In the Clerk's Office of the District Court of the District of Massachusetts.

TO

## F. ORMOND J. S. BAZIN

This Book

## IS RESPECTFULLY DEDICATED,

BY HIS FRIEND

WILLIAM T. ADAMS.

# PREFACE.

THIS volume, the fifth of "THE ARMY AND NAVY STORIES," is not a biography of the distinguished soldier whose *sobriquet* in the army has been chosen as its principal title, though the prominent incidents of his military career are noticed in its pages. The writer offers his humble tribute of admiration to the energetic and devoted general who will be recognized under the appellation given to this work; but perhaps the object of the volume may be better represented by the second title. It follows Tom Somers, "The Soldier Boy" and "The Young Lieutenant," in his brilliant and daring career as a staff officer, through some of the most stormy and trying scenes of the late war.

As in the volumes of the series which have preceded it, the best sources of information upon military events have been carefully consulted; and to the extent to which the book is properly historical, it is intended to be faithful in its delineations. But the work is more correctly a record of personal adventure, no more complicated, daring, and romantic than may be found in the experience of many, who, through trial and tribulation, through victory and defeat, have passed from the inception to the gigantic failure of this gigantic rebellion.

More earnest than any other purpose in the production of the book, it has been the object of the writer to exhibit a character in his hero worthy the imitation of the boy and the man who may read it; and if it does not inculcate a lofty patriotism, and a noble and Christian morality, it will have failed of the highest aim of the author.

With the still stronger expression of gratitude which the increasing favor bestowed upon previous efforts demands of me, I pass the fifth volume of the series into the hands of my indulgent friends, hoping that it will not fall short of their reasonable expectations.

WILLIAM T. ADAMS.

# CONTENTS.

| CHAPTER | | PAGE |
|---|---|---|
| I. | A Fighting Man. | 11 |
| II. | A Skirmish on the Road. | 22 |
| III. | Fighting Joe. | 33 |
| IV. | Miss Maud Hasbrouk. | 44 |
| V. | The Boot on One Leg. | 55 |
| VI. | The Boot on the Other Leg. | 66 |
| VII. | South Mountain. | 77 |
| VIII. | Before the Great Battle. | 88 |
| IX. | Between the Pickets. | 98 |
| X. | Major Riggleston. | 109 |
| XI. | Shot in the Head. | 120 |
| XII. | The Council of Officers. | 131 |
| XIII. | The Battle of Antietam. | 141 |
| XIV. | The Battle on the Right. | 151 |
| XV. | After the Battle. | 161 |
| XVI. | The Mystery explained. | 171 |
| XVII. | Down in Tennessee. | 181 |
| XVIII. | The Guerillas at Supper. | 191 |
| XIX. | Tippy the Scout. | 202 |
| XX. | Skinley the Texan. | 213 |
| XXI. | The House of the Union Man. | 223 |

|       |                                        |     |
|-------|----------------------------------------|-----|
| XXII. | THE GREENBACK TRAIN. | 234 |
| XXIII. | THE BATTLE IN THE CLOUDS. | 244 |
| XXIV. | PEACH-TREE CREEK. | 254 |
| XXV. | THE MONKEY AND THE CAT'S PAW. | 264 |
| XXVI. | SUPPER FOR SEVEN. | 274 |
| XXVII. | THE CATS'S PAW TOO SHARP FOR THE MONKEY. | 284 |
| XXVIII. | THE BLOOD-HOUNDS ON THE TRACK. | 294 |
| XXIX. | THE PILGRIMAGE TO THE SEA. | 303 |
| XXX. | MAJOR SOMERS AND FRIENDS. | 314 |

# FIGHTING JOE.

# FIGHTING JOE;

OR,

## THE FORTUNES OF A STAFF OFFICER.

---

## CHAPTER I.

### A FIGHTING MAN.

"WELL, Alick, I don't know where I am," said Captain Thomas Somers, of the staff of the major general commanding the first army corps of the Army of the Potomac, then on its march to repel the invasion of Maryland, which had been attempted by the victorious rebels under General Lee.

"Well, massa, I'm sure I don't know," replied Alick, his colored servant. "If you was down 'bout Petersburg, I reckon I'd know all 'bout it."

"We must find out very soon," added Captain Somers, as he reined in his horse at a point where two roads branched off, one to the north-west and the other to the south-west.

"Day ain't no house 'bout here, massa."

"I don't want to lose my way, for I have no time to spare."

"Dar's somebody comin' up behind, massa," said Alick, who first heard the sounds of horses' feet approaching in the direction from which they had just come.

Captain Somers, after receiving the agreeable intelligence of his appointment on the staff of the general, in whose division he had served on the Peninsula, hastened to Washington to report for duty. He had hardly time to visit his friends, and was obliged to content himself with a short call on Miss Lilian Ashford, though he had an invitation to spend the evening with the family, extended for the purpose of enabling the young gentleman to cultivate an acquaintance with the beautiful girl's grandmother!

Lilian's father's mother was certainly a very estimable old lady, and her granddaughter loved and reverenced her with a fervor which was almost enthusiastic. It was quite natural, therefore, that she should wish Captain Somers, — for whom she had knit a pair of socks, which had been no small portion of his inspiration in the hour of battle, and for whom she had contracted a friendship, — it was quite natural that she should wish to have the captain well acquainted with her grandmother. She loved the old lady herself, and of course so brave, handsome, and loyal a person as her friend had proved to be, must share her reverence and respect. Besides, the venerable woman remembered all about the last war with Great Britain. Her husband had been one of the firemen sent out with axes to cut away the bridges which connect Boston with the surrounding country, when an invasion of the town was expected. She could tell a good story, and as Somers was a military man, it was highly important that he should know all about the dreaded invasion which did not take place.

Captain Somers was obliged to deprive himself of the pleasure of listening to the old lady's history of those stirring events, for more exciting ones were in progress on the very day of which we write. He was sorry, for he anticipated a great deal of pleasure from the visit, though whether he expected to derive the whole of it from the presence of the grandmother, we are not informed; and it would be wicked to pry too deeply into the secrets of the young man's heart. We are not quite sure that Lilian was entirely unselfish when she described what a rich treat the old lady's narrative would be; but we are certain that she was entirely sincere, and that it was quite proper to offer some extra inducement to secure the gallant captain's attendance.

The captain did not need any extraordinary inducements, beyond the presence of the fair Lilian herself. We even believe that he would have cheerfully spent the evening at No. — Rutland Street, if there had been no one but herself to give him a welcome, and aid him in passing away the hours. Nothing but a high sense of duty could have led him to break the engagement. The rebel hordes, victorious before Washington, and elated by the signal successes they had won, were pouring into Maryland, menacing Washington, Baltimore, and Philadelphia. It was a time which tried the souls of patriotic men — a time when no man who loved his country could rest in peace while there was a work which his hands could do.

The young staff officer called upon the lady and stated his situation. She blushed, as she always did in his presence, and gave him a God-speed on his patriotic mission. She hoped he would not be killed, or even wounded; that his feeble health would be restored; and that God would bless him as he went forth to do battle for his treason-ridden land. She was pale when he took her hand at parting; her bosom heaved with emotions, to which Somers found a response in his own heart, but which he could not explain.

He went to Washington; but the gallant army, still suffering from the pangs of recent defeat, but yet strong in the cause they had espoused, had marched to the scene of new battles. Somers had already provided himself with his staff uniform, and he remained in Washington only long enough to purchase two horses, one of which he mounted himself, while Alick rode the other, and started for the advance of the army. The roads were so cumbered with artillery trains and baggage wagons that his progress was very slow, and the corps to which he now belonged was several days in advance of him. By the advice of a general officer, he had made a détour from the direct road, and passed through a comparatively quiet country.

The rebels were at Frederick City, and their cavalry, in large and small bodies, was scattered all over the region, gathering supplies for the half starved, half clothed men of Lee's army. Thus far Somers had met none of these marauders, nor any of the guerillas, who, without a license from either side, were plundering soldiers and civilians who could offer no resistance. Somers had ridden as rapidly as his feeble state of health would permit; but his enthusiasm had urged him forward until his horse was more in danger of giving out than the rider. But when he reached the cross-roads, at which we find him, doubtful about the right way, he had slept the preceding night at a farm-house, and horse and rider were now in excellent condition.

"Are your pistols ready for use, Alick?" asked Somers, as he heard the sounds of the horses' feet.

"Yes, sar; always keep the pistols ready. But what you gwine to do wid pistols here?" replied the servant, as he took his weapon from his pocket.

"The country is full of rebels and guerillas; they may want our horses, and perhaps ourselves. I can't spare my coat and boots very well at present."

"Guess not, massa," laughed Alick, as he examined the lock of his pistol.

"I have never seen you in a fight, Alick. Do you think you can stand up to it?"

"Well, massa, I don't want to say much about that, but I reckon I won't run away no faster 'n you do."

"If I get into trouble with these ruffians, I shall want to know whether I can depend on you, or not."

"Golly, massa! You can depend on me till the cows come home!" exclaimed Alick. "I doesn't like to say much about it, but if these yere hossmen wants to fight, I'm not the chile to run away."

"They don't look much like rebels or guerillas," added Somers, as he obtained his first view of the approaching horsemen. "But you can't tell much by the looks in these times, for the villains have robbed us till half of them wear our own colors. Those people certainly wear the uniform of our army."

"Dar's only two of 'em, massa. I reckon they don't want to fight much."

"I only wished to be cautious; very likely they are loyal and true men," replied Somers, as the strangers came too near to permit any further remarks in regard to their probable character.

Both the travellers were evidently officers of the army, though, as Somers had suggested, it was impossible to tell what anybody was by the looks, or even if he was seen to take the oath of allegiance. As they came round a bend of the road, and discovered the captain and his servant, they reined up their steeds, and seemed to be disturbed by the same doubts which had troubled the first party. But they advanced, after a cautious survey, and each of them touched his cap, when they came within speaking distance. Somers politely returned the salute, and moved his horse towards them.

"Good morning, gentlemen," said he. "Can you inform me which is the road to Frederick City?"

"The left, sir. If you are going in that direction, we shall be glad of your company," replied one of the officers.

"Thank you; I shall be glad to go with you."

"I see by your uniform that you belong on the staff," added the officer who had done the talking.

"Yes, sir;" and Somers, without reserve, informed him who and what he was.

"Somers!" exclaimed the stranger. "I have heard of you before. Perhaps you remember one Dr. Scoville, of Petersburg?"

"Perfectly," laughed Somers.

"Well, sir, he is an uncle of mine."

"Indeed? I took you to be an officer of the United States army."

"So I am; but my father married a sister of Dr. Scoville."

"Dr. Scoville is a very good sort of man, but he is an awful rebel. I suppose he bears no good will towards me and my friend Major de Banyan."

"Perhaps not; but the affair was a capital joke on the doctor. And since he is a rebel, and a very pestilent one too, I enjoyed it quite as much as you did."

"I feel very grateful to him for what he did for me. I went into his house without an invitation; he dressed my wound, and nearly cured me. When the soldiers came upon us, he promised to give us up at the proper time, and pledged himself for our safety. We left him, one day, rather shabbily, I confess; but we had no taste for a rebel prison, for the rebs don't always manage their prisons very well."

"I have heard the whole story. It's rich. If you please, we will move on."

"With all my heart, major," replied Somers, who read his rank from his shoulder-straps.

"I am Major Riggleston, of the —nd Maryland Home Brigade, on detached duty, just now."

"I am glad to know you, Major Riggleston, especially as you are a relative of my friend Dr. Scoville, and on the right side."

"This is Captain Barkwood, of the regulars."

Somers saluted the quiet gentleman, who had hardly

spoken during the interview. Major Riggleston was dressed in an entirely new uniform, and rode a splendid horse, which led Somers to believe that he belonged to one of the wealthy and aristocratic families of the state which so tardily embraced the cause of the Union. On the other hand, Captain Barkwood looked as though he had seen hard service; for his uniform was rusty, and his face was bronzed by exposure beneath the fervid sun of the south.

The party were excellently well acquainted with each other before they had ridden a mile. After the topics suggested by the first meeting had been exhausted, Somers mentioned his fear of the guerillas and rebel marauders, who kept a little way in advance of the invading army. The travellers were now farther north than Frederick, and some distance from the advancing line of the Union army. The road they had chosen was not one of the great thoroughfares of the state; consequently it was but little frequented.

" I don't object to meeting a small party of guerillas," said Major Riggleston; "for, gentlemen, if you are of the same mind that I am, we should show them the quality of true Union steel."

" I hope we shall not meet any; but if we do, I am in no humor to lose my horse or my boots," replied Somers. "But we may meet so many of them that it would be better to trust to our horses' heels than to the quality of our steel."

"True — too many would not be agreeable; but, say a dozen or twenty of them. We could whip that number without difficulty. The fact is, gentlemen, I am a fighting man. There has been too much of this looking at the enemy, and then running away. I repeat, gentlemen, I am a fighting man."

"I am glad to hear it, and glad to have met you, for I am told there are a good many of these small plundering parties loose about this region; and I would rather fight than lose my boots," laughed Somers.

"Three of us can do a good thing," added the major.

"Four," suggested Somers.

"Four?"

"My man can fight."

"But he is a nigger; niggers won't fight."

"He will. By the way, he came from your uncle's, at Petersburg."

"Alick!" exclaimed the major, glancing back at the servant.

He did not seem to be well pleased to discover one of his uncle's contrabands at this distance from home; for, with many other chivalrous southrons, he believed it would be a good thing to preserve the Union, if slavery could be preserved with it. He spoke a few words to Alick, but did not seem to enjoy the interview.

"Yes, we can whip at least twenty of the villains," added the major, as he resumed his place between

Somers and Captain Barkwood. "What do you think?" he continued, turning to the regular.

"I hope we shall not meet any. I am a coward by nature. I would rather run than fight, any time," replied the captain. "Of all things I dislike these small skirmishes, these hand-to-hand fights."

"I like them; I'm a fighting man," said the major.

"I'm afraid you will have a chance to test your mettle," said Somers. "Those fellows are guerillas, if I mistake not," added he, pointing to half a dozen horsemen who were approaching them.

## CHAPTER II.

#### A SKIRMISH ON THE ROAD.

THE horsemen who had attracted the attention of Captain Somers were hard-looking fellows. They were dressed in a miscellaneous manner, their clothes being partly civilian and partly military. Portions of their garb were new, and probably at no distant period had been part of the stock in trade of some industrious clothier in one of the invaded towns; and portions were faded and dilapidated, bearing the traces of a severe march through the soft mud of Virginia. It was not easy to mistake their character.

The guerillas perceived the approaching party almost as soon as they were themselves perceived. They adopted no uncertain tactics, but instantly put spurs to their horses and galloped up to the little squad of officers. They appeared to have no doubts whatever in regard to the issue of the meeting, for they resorted to no cautionary movements, and made no prudential halts. They had evidently had everything their own way in previous encounters of this description, and seemed to be satisfied that they had only to demand an unconditional surrender in order to find their way at once to the pockets of the travellers, or to appropriate their coats and boots to the use of the rebel army.

"Halt!" said the nondescript gentleman at the head of the guerillas.

"Your business?" demanded Major Riggleston.

"Sorry to trouble you, gentlemen, but you are my prisoners," said the chief guerilla, as blandly as though he had been in a drawing-room.

"Who are you, gentlemen?" asked the major.

"I don't like to be uncivil to a well-dressed gentleman like yourself; but I haven't learned my catechism lately, and can't stop to be questioned. In one word, do you surrender?"

"Allow me a moment to consult my friends."

"Only one moment."

"Don't you think we had better surrender, Captain Somers?"

"I thought you were a fighting man," replied Somers.

"I am, when circumstances will admit of it; but they are two to our one."

"Just now you thought we were a match for at least twenty of these fellows."

"Time's up, gentlemen," said the dashing guerilla.

"What do you say, Captain Somers?"

"You can do as you please; I don't surrender, for one,"

"But this is madness."

"I don't care what it is; I am going to fight my way through."

"Do you surrender?" demanded the impatient chief of the horsemen.

"No!" replied Somers, in his most decided tone.

"Then you are a dead man!" And the guerilla raised his pistol.

Somers already had one of his revolvers in his hand, and before the villain had fairly uttered the words, he presented his weapon and fired, as quick as the flash of the lightning. The leader dropped from his horse, and his pistol was discharged in the act, but the ball went into the ground. Almost at the same instant the quiet captain of the regulars fired, and wounded another of the banditti. The others, apparently astonished at this unexpected resistance, discharged their pistols, and pressed forward, with their sabres in hand, to avenge the fall of their comrades.

Somers rapidly fired the other barrels of his revolver, and so did Captain Barkwood, but without the same decisive effect as before, though two of the assailants appeared to be slightly wounded. There was no further opportunity to use firearms, and the officers drew their swords, as they fell back before the impetuous charge of the savage guerillas. Major Riggleston followed their example, and for a moment the sparks flew from the well-tempered steel of the combatants. Our officers were accomplished swordsmen, but the furious rebels appeared to be getting the better of them. Major Riggleston contrived to wheel his horse, and was so fortunate as to get out of the mêlée with a whole skin.

At this point, when victory seemed about to perch on the rebel standard, Alick, who had thus far been ignored, brought down a third guerilla with his pistol. The negro was cool, collected, and self-possessed. He had not fired before, because the officers stood between him and the assailants. Now, as he had no sword, he stood off, and took deliberate aim at his man.

Captain Barkwood, who was a man of immense muscle, succeeded, after a desperate hand-to-hand conflict, in wounding his opponent in the sword arm. The fellow dropped his weapon, and turning his horse, fled with the utmost precipitation. The only remaining one, finding himself alone, immediately followed his example. The battle was won, and the coats and boots were evidently saved.

"Why don't you follow them?" cried Major Riggleston, rushing madly up to the spot at this decisive moment. "Hunt them down! Tear them to pieces."

"We'll leave that for our fighting man to do," replied Somers, with a smile, though he was so much out of breath with the violence of his exertions that he could scarcely articulate the words.

"Don't let them escape," added the major, furiously. "Cut them down! Don't let them plunder the country any more."

As he spoke, he put spurs to his horse, and dashed madly up the road in pursuit of the defeated guerillas.

"Your hand, Captain Somers," said the regular. "You are a trump."

"Thank you; and I am happy to reciprocate the compliment," replied the young staff officer, as he took the proffered hand of Captain Barkwood.

"As a general rule, I don't think much of volunteer officers," continued the regular; "but you are a stunning good fellow, and as plucky as a hen that has lost one of her chickens."

"I am obliged to you for your good opinion, and especially for your ornithological simile," laughed Somers, who, we need not add, was delighted with the conduct of his companion.

"My what?"

"Your ornithological simile."

"My dear fellow, you must have swallowed a quarto dictionary. If you had only used that expression before the fight, the rebels would certainly have run away, and declined to engage a man who used words of such ominous length. No matter; you can fight."

"I can when I am obliged to do so. You remarked, a little while ago, that you were a coward by nature."

"So I am; but it was safer to fight than it was to run."

"You did not behave like a man who is a coward by nature."

"But I am a coward; and I dislike these hand-to-hand encounters."

"You didn't appear to dislike them very much just now," added Somers, who was filled with admiration at the gallant bearing of the regular.

"I do; war is a science. I play at it just as I do at chess. By the way, Captain Somers, do you play chess?"

"Only a little."

"Well, it's a noble game; and I may have the pleasure of letting you beat me some time. War is like chess; it's a great game. I like to see a well-planned battle, and even to take a part in it. But these little affairs, where everything depends on brute force, are my particular abomination. There is no science about them — no strategy — no chance to flank, or do any other smart thing."

"Here comes the major; he didn't catch his man," said Somers, as the "fighting man" was seen galloping towards them.

"He's a prudent man," replied the regular, hardly betraying the contempt he felt for this particular volunteer.

"He's a Maryland man."

"So am I," promptly returned Captain Barkwood, as though he feared that something might be said against the bravery of the men of his state. "I was born and brought up not ten miles from the spot where we now stand."

"Why didn't you follow me?" demanded the major, in a reproachful tone, as he reined in his panting steed.

"We had got enough of it," answered the regular.

"We might have brought them down if you had joined me in the pursuit."

"We might, if you had stuck by us in the fight," said Somers, with a gentle smile, to break the force of the rebuke.

"Stood by you?" exclaimed Major Riggleston, his face flushed with anger. "Do you intend to insinuate that I did not stand by you?"

"You did, but at a safe distance."

"Didn't I do all the talking with the villains?" foamed the major.

"Certainly you did," replied the regular.

"Didn't I bear the whole brunt of the assault at the beginning?"

"Undoubtedly you did," responded Captain Barkwood, before Somers could speak a word.

"Didn't I fight like a tiger, till—"

"Unquestionably you did."

"Till my rein got entangled in my spur, and whirled my horse round?"

"My dear major, you behaved like a lion," said Barkwood, in tones so soothing that the anger of Riggleston passed away like the shadow of a summer cloud.

"I am a fighting man."

"That's so."

"And I dislike this marching and countermarching in the face of an enemy."

"There we unfortunately disagree for the first time. That is strategy, — the art of war, — and all that makes war glorious."

"I believe in pitching into an enemy, and, when he is beaten, in following him up till there is nothing left of him. I regret, gentlemen, that you did not join in the pursuit of the two miscreants with me. We might have annihilated them as well as not."

Somers did not understand the humor of the regular, and could not fathom his object in permitting the coward still to believe that he was a fighting man. While the conversation was in progress, Alick had removed the bodies of the two dead rebels from the road, and placed the other two, who were severely wounded, in a comfortable position under a tree. He had filled their canteens with water from the brook which ran across the road a short distance from the spot, and left them to live or die, as the future might determine. He had also transferred a good saddle from one of the guerillas' horses to his own animal, which had not before been provided with one.

The party moved on again. Major Riggleston talked about the fight; for some reason or other he could speak of nothing else. He still called himself a fighting man, and still talked as though he had fired the most effective shots and struck the hardest blows which had been given. The regular agreed with him in all things, except when he impugned the sacred claims of strategy.

"Never cross a fool in his folly, nor ruin a man in his own estimation," said Captain Barkwood, when Somers, at a favorable moment, asked an explanation of his singular commendation of the poltroon.

"But he is a coward."

"Call no man a coward but yourself. There is hardly an officer in the army, from the general-in-chief down to the corporal of the meanest regiment in the service, that has not been called a coward. You don't know who are cowards, and who are not."

"Perhaps you are right."

"I know I am. I am a coward myself, but I know nothing about anybody else."

"I differ with you."

"You don't know anything about it. The major don't love you over much now for what you hinted. Never make an enemy when there is no need of it."

The approach of Major Riggleston put an end to this conversation. Somers could not help noticing that the major treated him rather cavalierly; but as he was not particularly anxious to secure the esteem of such a man, the manner of his companion did not disturb him.

In the afternoon the party reached Frederick, which had just been abandoned by Lee's rear guard, and was now occupied by a portion of McClellan's advance.

"Gentlemen, we have had a hard ride, and I know you must be tired as well as myself," said Major Riggleston, as they entered the city. "You will permit me to offer you the hospitalities of my father's house."

"Thank you; I accept, for one," replied Captain Barkwood. "I am not tired, but I am half starved."

"And you, Somers?" added the major, with a degree of cordiality in his manner which he had not exhibited since the skirmish on the road.

The young captain had been in the saddle all day; his health was feeble, and he was very much exhausted by the journey. He had hoped to reach the headquarters of the first army corps that night; but he was still several miles distant from his destination, and his physical condition did not admit of this addition to his day's travel. With many thanks he accepted the invitation, apparently so cordially extended, and the little party halted, soon after, in the grounds of an elegant mansion. The tired horses were given into the keeping of the servants, and Major Riggleston led the way into the house.

They were ushered into the drawing-room, where the major excused himself to inform the family of their arrival. He left the door open behind him.

"They are Yankee officers!" exclaimed a female voice. "What did Fred bring them here for? Get out of sight, Ernest, as fast as you can."

A door leading from the entry closed, and the visitors heard no more. The regular paid no attention to the remark, and Somers followed his example.

## CHAPTER III.

### FIGHTING JOE.

CAPTAIN SOMERS, though he said nothing to his companion about the remark to which they had listened, could not help thinking about it. The regular and himself had been alluded to as Yankee officers. It was evident that some one was present who ought not to be present; but as a guest in the house, it was not competent for him to investigate the meaning of the suspicious words.

Major Riggleston presently returned to the drawing-room, attended by an elderly gentleman, whom he introduced as his father, and a beautiful but majestic and haughty young lady of eighteen, whom he introduced as Miss Maud Hasbrouk. When Somers heard her voice, which was as musical as the rippling of a mountain rill, he recognized the tones of the person who had used the doubtful words in the adjoining room.

The old gentleman was happy to see the visitors, especially as they belonged to the Union army, whose presence was welcome to him after the visit of the rebels. He hoped that General McClellan would be able to drive the invaders from the soil — conquer, capture, and exterminate them. His words were certainly strong enough to vouch for his loyalty; and these, added to the fact that the major was an officer in the Maryland Home Brigade, satisfied Somers that he had not fallen into a nest of rebels and traitors, as the obnoxious remark, not intended for his ears, had almost led him to believe.

"The more true men we have here the better; for we have been completely overrun by traitors," said the old gentleman, alluding to the visit of Lee's army.

"You use strong words, Mr. Riggleston," added the lady, whose bright eyes flashed as she spoke.

"I say what I mean," continued the host.

"Is there any doubt of the fact that the state has been invaded by the rebels?" asked Somers, with a smile.

"None whatever; but Mr. Riggleston called them traitors," replied Miss Hasbrouk.

"Is there any doubt of that fact?"

"Are men who are fighting for the dearest rights of man traitors?" demanded she, warmly.

"Undoubtedly not. But the rebels are not fighting for any such thing."

"I beg your pardon, Captain Somers. I think they are. Permit me to add, that I am a rebel."

"I am very sorry to hear it," laughed Somers, pleased with the spirit, no less than the beauty, of the lady.

"I suppose you are," replied she. "The South is fighting for the right of self-government — for its own existence. The right of secession is just as evident to me as the right to live."

The question of secession was fully discussed by the lady and Somers, but both of them were in the best of humor. Neither contestant succeeded in convincing the other on a single point; and when the party were called to supper, they had advanced just about as far as the statesmen had when the momentous issue was handed over to the arbitrament of arms. It was a matter to be adjusted by hard fighting; and as Miss Hasbrouk and Somers did not intend to settle the question in this rude manner, the subject was dropped.

The family, so far as Somers could judge, were loyal people. The imperial young lady, who was a fit type of the southern character, was only a visitor. In spite of her proud and haughty bearing, she was a very agreeable person, and the guests enjoyed her society.

"I am a rebel," said she, as they sat down to supper; "but I am, sorely against my will, I confess, a non-combatant, and we are now on neutral ground. We will bury our differences, then, Captain Somers, and be friends."

"With all my heart," replied the gallant young captain.

A very pleasant evening was spent in the drawing-room, during which Miss Hasbrouk affected the company of Somers rather than that of the regular, who appeared to be as stoical in society as he was on the road. She was lively, witty, and fascinating, and seemed to be very much delighted with the society of the young staff officer. He was an exceedingly good-looking fellow, it is true; but he was a Yankee, and she made no secret of her aversion to Yankees in general. He was an exception to the rule, and she compelled him to relate the history of his brief campaign at Petersburg. She laughed at the chagrin of Dr. Scoville, when his invalid took to himself wings and flew away; but she took no pains to conceal her sympathy with the cause of the Confederacy.

At an early hour the officers retired; and as they announced their intention to depart at daylight in the morning, they took leave of the ladies. Miss Hasbrouk was so kind as to hope she might meet the captain again; for notwithstanding his vile political affinities, he was a sensible person.

Before the sun rose, Somers and the regular were in the saddle. The major, whose route lay in a different direction, was no longer their companion. The headquarters of the first army corps were on the Monocacy; and thither the travellers wended their way through a beautiful country, which excited the admiration even of the stoical captain of the regulars, though it was no new scene to him.

The reveille was sounding in the camps of the Pennsylvania Reserves as they passed through on their way to the tent of the commanding general. They reached their destination, and their names were sent in by an orderly in attendance.

"Captain Somers, I am glad to see you," said the general, at a later hour, when they obtained an audience.

"Thank you, general; I am very grateful for the kindness and consideration you have bestowed upon me," replied Somers.

"You are an aid-de-camp now; but I ought to say that I gave you the appointment because you are a good fellow on a scout."

"I will do my best in whatever position you may place me."

"You were rather unfortunate in your last trip, but you accomplished the work I gave you to do. We shall do some hard fighting in a day or two, and there will be sharp work for you before that comes off."

"I am ready, general. Every man is ready to march or fight as long as he can stand while you are in command."

"I will see you again in an hour, Somers," said the general, as he turned to Captain Barkwood, who belonged to the engineers, and had been assigned to a position on the staff.

Somers soon made the acquaintance of the general's

"military family." His position and rank were defined in the general orders, and duly promulgated. From those around him he obtained all the current knowledge in regard to the situation of the rebel army, which was posted in the Catoctin valley, with the South Mountain range in the rear, whose gaps and passes it was to defend.

At the time appointed Captain Somers again stood in the presence of the general, who was his beau-ideal of all that was grand and heroic in the military chieftain. He was a tall, straight, well-formed man, with a ruddy complexion, flecked with little thready veins, and a muscular frame. His eye was full of energy; he spoke with his eye as much as with his voice. His military history was familiar to the nation. He was a decided man, and his decision had won him his first appointment in the army. He said what he meant, and meant what he said. His energy of character had made him a success from the beginning. His faith in himself and his faith in the loyal army were unbounded. He fought and conquered by the force of his mighty will. He attempted only what was possible, and triumphed through the faith of an earnest soul. His military judgment was of the highest order, and when he had decided what could be done, he did it. His conclusions, however suddenly reached, were not the offspring of impulse; they were carefully drawn from well-founded premises. His quick eye and his solid judgment rapidly collated all the facts in regard to an enemy's strength, relative situation, and advantage of position; and from them he promptly deduced the conclusion whether to fight or not — how, when, and where to fight.

The general's pet name was " Fighting Joe ; " and by this appellation he was known and loved in the army. But he was not a rash man; he made no unconsidered movements. If the term implies rashness and blundering impetuosity, it is a misnomer; but, after Williamsburg, Glendale, Malvern, South Mountain, Antietam, Lookout Mountain, who could mistake its meaning? for his battles were too uniformly successful to be the issues of merely headlong courage and unmatured strategy. All his operations on the splendid fields where he has so gloriously distinguished himself, exhibit a head as well as an arm; carefully considered plan, as well as bold and determined execution.

The mention of " Fighting Joe " warmed the hearts of the soldiers. He was more popular than any other general in the army. Our soldiers were thinking men, as well as brave ones. They could not love and honor a general who led them into the forefront of battle to be entrapped and sacrificed. They could not believe in a man whose highest recommendation was brute courage. " Fighting Joe " was one of the ablest strategists in the army; and, wherever he has justified his title as a fighting man, he has also displayed the highest skill and judgment, and a profound knowledge and appreciation of the science of war.

Somers stood before the general with a certain feeling of awe and reverence, which one experiences in the presence of a truly great man. There was no time to talk of the past, for the present and the future were full of trials and cares — were full of a nation's life and hope. Fighting Joe was cool and self-possessed, as he always was, even in the mad rage of the hottest fight; but he was earnest and anxious. He was even now doing that work which wins battles quite as much as the fiery onslaught.

Burnside was in command of the right wing of the army, which occupied the vicinity of Frederick. The rebels had just been driven out of Middletown, and the cannon was roaring beyond Catoctin Creek; but it was evident to the general that no pitched battle could take place that day. He wanted certain information, which he thought Captain Somers was smart enough to procure for him. A map lay on the table in the tent, and in a few telling words he explained what he wanted.

"Don't be rash, Somers," said he, as the aid-de-camp rose to depart. "Intelligent courage is what we want. I shall depend upon you for skill and discretion as well as dash and boldness."

"I will do the best I can," replied the captain, as he left the tent and mounted his horse.

He dashed off towards Middletown, as the army commenced its march in the same direction. He reached this place before noon, and agreeably to his instructions, pursued a northerly course, until he reached a point beyond the active operations of Pleasanton's cavalry, which was scouring the country. Leaving his horse at a farm-house, he advanced on foot to the westward of the creek, until he discovered the outposts of the rebel army. Small squads of Confederate cavalry were beating about this region, and Somers was obliged to dodge them several times. But he obtained his information, and fully acquainted himself with the nature of the country, and the situation of the rebels to the north of the Cumberland road.

It was three o'clock in the afternoon when he had completed his reconnoissance, and he was nearly exhausted by the long walk he had taken, and the excitement of his occupation. He was at least two miles from the farm-house where he had left his horse. He had eaten nothing since breakfast, and he was faint for the want of food. He walked one mile, and stopped to rest near an elegant mansion, which evidently belonged to one of the grandees of Maryland. He was tempted to visit the house and procure some refreshment; but, as he was alone, and knew nothing of the political status of the occupants, he did not deem it prudent to do so.

After resting a short time, he rose and continued his weary walk towards the farm-house. As he passed the door of the elegant mansion, a chaise stopped at the gate, and a young officer handed a lady from the vehicle. A servant led the horse away. The lady paused at the gate, and appeared to be observing him. Somers could think of no reason why the lady should watch him, and he continued on his course till he came within a few feet of the spot where she stood.

"Captain Somers!" exclaimed she; "I am delighted to see you again so soon."

"Miss Hasbrouk," replied he, not a little surprised to find in her his rebel friend, whom he had met in Frederick the preceding evening.

"This is an unexpected pleasure," added she, extending her hand, which the young man took.

"I should hardly have expected to meet you at this distance from Frederick."

"O, I reside here; this is my father's house. You are some distance from the Yankee army."

"As you are a rebel, it is hardly proper for me to inform you why I happen to be here," laughed he. "I am an invalid, and am walking for my health."

"It is well you are away from your army, for they will all be captured in a few days."

"Perhaps not; but I shall be with the army before night."

"This is Major Riggleston," said she, turning to the gentleman, who had followed the servant to the stable, and had just returned.

"How do you do, again, major?" said Somers.

"Happy to meet you, Captain Somers," replied the major, not very cordially.

"Now you must come into the house, Captain Somers. It is just dinner time with us," continued the lady.

Somers was too faint and hungry to refuse.

## CHAPTER IV.

### MISS MAUD HASBROUK.

THE lady conducted Captain Somers to the sitting-room of the house. He was followed by Major Riggleston, who, judging by his looks and actions, regarded the staff officer with no special favor. Miss Hasbrouk did all the talking, however, and seemed to do it for the purpose of keeping the major in the shade, for she carefully turned aside two or three observations he made, as though they were of no consequence, or as though they might provoke an unpleasant discussion.

"I am particularly delighted to meet you again, Captain Somers," said the imperial beauty, as they entered the apartment.

"Thank you," replied he; though he could see no good reason why Miss Maud Hasbrouk should be particularly delighted to see him.

He was a Union man and a loyal soldier, while she was a rebel, with strength of mind enough to regret that her sex compelled her to be a non-combatant. She was a magnificent creature, even to Somers, whose knowledge of the higher order of beauties that float about in the mists of fashionable society was very limited. She was fascinating, and he could not resist the charm of her society; albeit in the present instance he was too much exhausted by ill health and over-exertion to be very brilliant himself.

"This is very unexpected, considering the distance from the place at which I met you last evening," said he.

"O, it isn't a very great distance to Frederick. The major drove me over in three hours," replied she.

"Three and a half, Maud," interposed the major, apparently because he felt the necessity of saying something to avoid being regarded as a mere cipher.

"How do you feel to-day, after the little brush we had yesterday, major?" added Somers, turning to the gentleman.

"What brush do you refer to?" asked Major Riggleston, rather coldly.

"The little rub we had with the guerillas."

"Really, you have — "

"Now, gentlemen, will you excuse me for a few moments?" said Miss Hasbrouk, very impolitely breaking in upon the major's remark.

"Certainly," replied Somers, with his politest bow. "You are a fighting man, Major Riggleston; and the affair of yesterday was pretty sharp work for a few minutes."

"Of course I'm a fighting man; but —"

"Major, you promised me something, you will remember," said the lady, who still lingered in the room; "and now is the best time in the world to redeem your promise."

"What do you mean, Maud?" demanded the major.

"Why, don't you remember?"

"Upon my life I don't."

"Perhaps Captain Somers will excuse you for a few moments, while I refresh your memory."

"Certainly; to be sure," added the polite staff officer.

He moved towards the door at which the lady stood. Somers saw her whisper something to him as she took him familiarly by the arm.

"O, yes, I remember all about it now!" exclaimed he, with sudden vivacity. "I will return in a few moments, Captain Somers, if you will excuse me."

"By all means; don't let me interfere with any arrangement you have made."

They retired, and the door closed behind them. Somers was not a little befogged by the conduct of both the lady and the gentleman. Several times she had interrupted him, and the major had an astonishingly bad memory. He seemed not to remember even the skirmish on the road; and he was equally unmindful of what had passed between him and the lady at some period antecedent to the present.

They were quite intimate; and, slightly versed as the young officer was in affairs of love and matrimony, he had no difficulty in arriving at the conclusion that the interesting couple who had just left him were more than friends; and though he had not the skill to determine what particular point in the courtship they had reached, he ventured to believe they were engaged. Though it was rather a rash and unauthorized conclusion, it was a correct one; showing that young men know some things by intuition.

Somehow Major Riggleston did not appear exactly as he had appeared the preceding day. His uniform did not look quite so bright; his manner was more brusque and less polished; and he spoke with a heavier and more solid tone. But men are not always the same on one day that they are on another; and it was quite probable that the major was suffering for the want of his dinner, or from some vexation not apparent to the casual observer.

Somers wanted his dinner; not as an epicure is impatient for the feast which is to tickle his palate, but as a man who knows and feels that meat is strength. His health was not yet sufficiently established to enable him to endure the hardship of an empty stomach; for his muscles seemed, in his present weak state, to derive their power more directly than usual from that important organ. He did not, therefore, worry himself to obtain a solution of what was singular in the conduct of the lady and her lover.

They were absent but a few moments before the major returned. If he had been gone seven years, and passed through a Parisian polishing school in the interim, his tone and his manner could not have been more effectually changed. He looked and acted more like the Major Riggleston of yesterday. He was all suavity now; and, what was vastly more remarkable, his memory was as perfect as though he had made mnemonics the study of a lifetime. He remembered all about the skirmish on the road, and even recalled incidents connected with that affair of which Somers was profoundly ignorant.

"Captain Somers, that was the hardest fight for a little one I ever happened to be in," said the major, after the event had been thoroughly rehearsed.

"It was sharp for a few moments. By the way, major, what is your opinion of Alick now?" asked Somers.

"Well, I was rather surprised to see him go in as he did. He is a brave fellow."

"So he is; I did not know whether he would fight or not; but I thought he would."

"O, I was sure of it."

"Were you? Before the fight you seemed to be of the opinion that he was of no account."

"That was said concerning niggers in general. I always had a great deal of confidence in Alick. When he fired his gun I knew what the boy meant."

"His pistol, you mean; he had no gun."

"You are right; it was a pistol," said the major, with more confusion than this trifling inaccuracy justified.

"In the pursuit of the guerillas — "

"Yes, in the pursuit Alick was splendid," continued Riggleston, taking the words out of Somers's mouth.

"You forget, major; you conducted the pursuit alone," mildly added the staff officer.

"O, yes! so I did. I am mixing up this matter with another affair, in which my boy Mingo chased the Yankees — "

"Chased the what?" interposed Somers, confounded by this singular and inappropriate remark.

"The guerillas, I said," laughed the major. "What did you think I said?"

"I understood you to say the Yankees."

"O, no! Yankees? No; I am one myself. I said guerillas."

"If you did, I misunderstood you."

"Of course I didn't say Yankees. That is quite impossible."

Somers was disposed to be polite, even at the sacrifice of the point of veracity; therefore he did not contradict his companion, though he felt entirely certain in regard to the language used.

"Of course you could not have meant Yankees, whatever you said," added Somers.

"Certainly not. Do you know why I didn't catch those — those guerillas?" continued the major.

"I do not," replied Somers; but he had a strong suspicion that it was because he did not want to catch them; because it would have been imprudent for him to catch them; because it would have been in the highest degree dangerous for him to catch them.

"I'll tell you why I didn't catch them," added the major, rubbing his hands as a man does when he has a point to make. "It was because their horses went faster than mine."

"Good!" exclaimed Somers, who had the judgment to perceive that this answer was intended as a joke, and who was politic enough to render the homage due to such a tremendous effort — a laugh, as earnest as the circumstances would permit.

"Or possibly it was because my horse went slower than theirs," added the major, with the evident design of perpetrating a joke even more stupendous than the last.

We beg to suggest to our readers, young and old, that a person lays himself open more by his jokes, his puns, and his witticisms, than by any other means of communication between one soul and another with which we are acquainted. Hear a man talk about business, politics, morality, or religion, and you have a very inadequate idea of his moral and mental resources. Hear him jest, hear him make a pun, hear him indulge in a witticism, and you have his brains mapped out before you. We have heard a man get off a witticism, and felt an infinite contempt for him; we have heard a man get off a witticism, and felt a profound respect for him. It is not the thing said; it is not the manner in which it is said; it is not the look with which it is said. It is all three combined. He who would conceal himself from those around him should neither get drunk nor attempt to be funny.

Major Riggleston had revealed himself to Captain Somers more completely in that unguarded joke than in all that had passed between them before. The young staff officer was not a moral nor a mental philosopher; but that agonizing jest had given him a poorer opinion of his companion than he had before entertained. It was fortunate for the major that Miss Hasbrouk returned before he had an opportunity to launch another witticism upon the sea of the captain's charity, or the latter might have prematurely learned to despise him.

"We have not lately been honored by the voluntary presence of gentlemen at dinner, Captain Somers; and you will pardon me for lingering an extra moment before my glass," said the merry lady.

"Happy glass!" replied Somers.

"Thank you, captain; that was very pretty."

"Excellent!" added the major, who seemed to be hungering and thirsting for something funny or smart.

A bell rang in the hall, which Somers took to be the summons for dinner; and he was thankful, and took courage accordingly; for however much he enjoyed the society of the fascinating Maud, he could not forget that he owed a solemn duty to the outraged member of his body corporate, which had been kept fasting since an early breakfast hour.

"Now, gentlemen, shall I have the pleasure of conducting you to the dining-room?" continued Miss Hasbrouk.

"Thank you."

"Your arm, if you please, Captain Somers," said the brilliant lady.

Of course Somers complied with this reasonable request, though he had not been in the habit of observing these little courtesies at the cottage in Pinchbrook, nor even in some of the best regulated families at the Harbor, making no little pretensions to gentility. It seemed to him that it would have been more proper, in the present instance, and with the supposed relation between them, for the lady to take the arm of the gentleman to whom she was engaged; but he had not very recently read any book on the etiquette of good society, and he was utterly unable to settle the difficult question.

They passed through the hall and entered the dining-room. The table was laid for only three; and while Somers was wondering where the rest of the family were, a tremendous knocking was heard at the front door.

"Somebody is in earnest," said Maud. "He knocks like a sheriff who comes with authority. Take this seat, if you please, captain."

"Thank you, Miss Hasbrouk," replied Somers, as he took the appointed place.

"I hope that isn't any one after me," added the major, as he seated himself opposite to Somers. "I don't want to lose my dinner."

"You shall not lose it, major," answered Maud, as a colored servant entered the room with a salver in his hand, on which lay a letter.

"For Major Riggleston," said the man, as he presented the salver to him.

The major took the letter and broke the seal, apologizing to Somers for doing so. His eyes suddenly opened wider than their natural spread, and his chin dropped till mouth and eyes were both eloquent with astonishment. He sprang out of his chair, and assumed an attitude in the highest degree dramatic. Somers almost expected to hear him perpetrate a witticism.

"What is it, major?" demanded Maud, who seemed to be enduring the most agonizing suspense.

"I must go this instant!" exclaimed the major, still gazing at the momentous letter.

"What has happened?"

"Don't ask me, Maud," answered he, in excited tones. "I will be back before night; perhaps in an hour. You will excuse me, Captain Somers."

"Certainly," replied Somers.

The major rushed to the door, cramming the letter into his pocket, or attempting to do so, as he moved off. The document fell on the floor without the owner's notice.

"What can it mean?" said Maud, with a troubled look.

Somers did not know what it meant; if he had, it is doubtful whether he would have had the temerity to stop to dinner.

## CHAPTER V.

### THE BOOT ON ONE LEG.

"WHAT can have happened?" said Maud, apparently musing on the event which had just transpired. "The major is not often moved so deeply as he appeared to be just now."

"Something of importance, evidently," said Somers. "He has dropped the letter on the floor."

"So he has," said she, glancing at the document. "Thus far I have resisted the propensity of Mother Eve to know more than the law allows; and I think I will not yield to it now. It would hardly be honorable for me to read the letter after the major has declined to inform me what has occurred. But, whatever it may be, we will have some dinner."

Whatever opinions Somers may have entertained on some of the other points suggested by the fair hostess, he had none in regard to the last proposition. He was absolutely and heartily in favor of the dinner, without regard to Mother Eve's curiosity, or her favored representative then before him. The dinner was a good one, though the rebels had so recently gathered up all the provision which the country appeared to contain. With every mouthful that he ate Somers's strength seemed mysteriously to return to him.

The dinner was not so formal as might have been expected in the house of a Maryland grandee, and did not occupy over half an hour; but in that half hour he had grown strong and vigorous again, and felt equal to any emergency which might occur. However agreeable the society of the fascinating Maud had proved, he began to be very impatient for the moment when he could, without outraging the laws of propriety, break the spell which bound him. He had faithfully discharged his duty to the inner man, and he bethought him that he owed another and higher obligation to his country; that the commanding general of the first army corps was expecting to hear from him, though the time given him to complete his mission had not yet expired.

While he was considering some fit excuse with which to tear himself away from his interesting companion, — for it was not prudent to inform an avowed rebel lady that he had been engaged in collecting information for the use of a Union general, and must return to report the result of his mission, — while he was thinking what he should say to her, he heard something which sounded marvellously like the tramp of horses' feet on the walks which surrounded the mansion. These sounds might have been sufficient to create a tempest of alarm in his mind if he had not believed that he was far enough from the camps of the rebels to insure the estate from a visit of their cavalry. He did not know exactly where he was in relation to the line of either army; but he felt a reasonable assurance that he was out of the reach of danger from the enemy.

He listened, therefore, with tolerable coolness, to the clatter of the horses' feet, and finally concluded that the animals belonged to the estate. This conclusion, however, was soon unpleasantly disturbed by other and more suspicious sounds than the tramp of horses — sounds like the clatter and clang of cavalry equipments. More than this, Maud looked anxious and excited, when there appeared to be not the least reason for anxiety and excitement on her part.

"Won't you take another peach, captain?" said she, glancing uneasily at the window, and then at the door.

"No more, I thank you, Miss Hasbrouk," replied Somers. "You seem to be having more visitors."

"No, I think not," answered she, with assumed carelessness.

"What is the meaning of those sounds, then?"

"They are nothing; perhaps some of the servants leading the horses down to the meadow."

"Do your horses wear cavalry trappings, Miss Hasbrouk?"

"Not that I am aware of. Do you think there is any cavalry around the house?"

"I am decidedly of that opinion; and, with your permission, I will step out and learn the occasion of this visit," said he, rising from the table, and making sure that the two revolvers he wore in his belt were in working order.

"I beg you will not leave me, Captain Somers," remonstrated Maud.

"I only wish to ascertain what the cavalry are."

"I depend upon you for protection, captain," said she, as she rose from her seat at the table. "Ah, here comes some one, who will explain it all to you," she added, as the front door was heard to open rather violently.

"I think it won't need much explanation," replied Somers, as through the window he discovered two grayback cavalrymen. "It is quite evident that the house is surrounded by rebel cavalry."

At this moment the door of the dining-room opened, and Major Riggleston stalked into the apartment. He looked at Somers, and then at the lady. The troubled, astonished expression on his face when he went away had disappeared, and he wore what the staff officer could not help interpreting as a smile of triumph.

"Well, Maud, how is it now?" asked the major, as for the sixth time, at least, he glanced from Somers to her.

The brilliant beauty made no reply to this indefinite question. Instead of speaking as a civilized lady should when addressed by her accepted lover, she threw herself into a chair with an *abandon* which would have been creditable in a first lady in a first-class comedy, but which was highly discreditable in a first-class lady discharging only the duties of the social amenities in refined society. She threw herself into a chair, and laughed as though she had been suddenly seized with a fit of that playful species of hysterics which manifests itself in the cachinnatory tendency of the patient.

Somers was surprised. A less susceptible person than himself would have been surprised to see an elegant and accomplished lady laugh so violently, when there was apparently nothing in the world to laugh at. He could not understand it; a wiser and more experienced person than Somers could not understand it. He knew about Œdipus, and the Sphinx's riddle which he solved; but if Œdipus had been there, in that mansion of a Maryland grandee, Somers would have defied him to solve the riddle of Miss Maud Hasbrouk's inordinate, excessive, hysterical laughter. If Major Riggleston, from the great depository of unborn humor in his subtle brain, had launched forth one of the most tremendous of his thunderbolts of wit, the mystery would have solved itself. If the major had uttered anything but the most commonplace and easily interpreted remark, Somers might have believed that he had perpetrated a joke which he was not keen enough to perceive.

The house was surrounded by rebel cavalry; that was no joke to him; it could be no joke to the major, for he was an officer in the Maryland Home Brigade, "on detached service," and what proved dangerous or fatal to one must prove dangerous or fatal to the other. But Riggleston did not seem to be in the least disturbed by the circumstance that the house was environed by Confederate cavalry. He stood looking at his lady-love, as though he was waiting her next move in the development of the game.

"What are you laughing at, Maud?" asked he, when he had watched her until his own patience was somewhat tried, and that of Somers had become decidedly shaky.

"Isn't it funny?" gasped she, struggling for utterance between the spasms of laughter.

"Yes, it is, very funny," replied he, obediently, though it was quite plain that he did not regard the scene as so excruciatingly amusing as the lady did.

"Why don't you laugh, then?"

"I would if I had time; but I must proceed to business."

"Don't spoil the scene yet," said she, with difficulty.

"Hurry it up, then, Maud."

"Captain Somers," added she, repressing her laughter to a more reasonable limit, "I am your most obedient servant."

"Thank you, Miss Hasbrouk," replied he, beginning to apprehend, for the first time, that he was individually and personally responsible for the joke which had so excited the lady's risibles. "If you are, you will oblige me by informing me what you are laughing at."

The lady broke forth anew, and peal on peal of laughter rang through the room. Somers tried to think what he had said or done that was so astoundingly funny, satisfied that his humor would certainly make his fortune when given a wider field of operations. It was evident that it would not do for him to be as funny as he could thereafter in the presence of ladies, or one of them might yet die of hysterics.

"Do you really wish to know what I am laughing at, Captain Somers?" asked she, at another brief interval of apparent sanity.

"That is what I particularly desire."

"I am laughing at the situation. Do you know that there is something irresistibly ludicrous in situations, captain? I delight in situations — funny situations I mean."

"Really, I don't see anything very amusing in the present situation," replied the puzzled staff officer.

"Don't you, indeed? Well, I'm afraid you won't appreciate the situation from your stand-point. What a pity we haven't a photographer to give us the scene, for future inspection!"

"Well, Miss Hasbrouk, you seem to be making yourself very merry at my expense. I am happy to have afforded you so much amusement; but I fear I am still your debtor for the bountiful hospitality of your house."

"Don't mention it, captain; and you won't wish to mention it a few hours hence."

"I assure you I shall ever gratefully remember your kindness to me."

"Perhaps not," laughed the maiden.

"Captain Somers," interposed the major, "I think we have carried the joke far enough; and we will now proceed to the serious part of the business. In one word, you —"

"Stop, Major Riggleston, if you please," interrupted Maud. "This is my affair."

"Hurry it along a little faster, then, if you will, Maud. The people outside will get tired of waiting."

"Don't you interfere, major. You forget that you are a Union officer, belonging to the Maryland Home Brigade. Captain Somers insists that you are; and of course you are."

"Of course I am; I had almost forgotten that little circumstance," laughed the major.

"Well, Miss Hasbrouk, since you are to manage the affair, I will thank you to inform me what it all means," demanded Somers, with the least evidence of impatience in his tones.

"With the greatest pleasure; with a pleasure which you cannot yet appreciate, I will inform you all about it. But, my dear Captain Somers, in deference to a lady who has admired you, *fêted* you, dined you, you will answer a few questions which I shall propose to you, before I proceed to the explanation."

"Be in haste, Maud," said the major.

"Major Riggleston, if you hurry me, I shall be obliged to ask you to leave the room," answered she, with a resumption of the imperial dignity she had partially abandoned.

"I'm dumb, Maud."

"Keep so, then. Now, Captain Somers, you are one of the heroes of the Yankee army; a down-east pink of chivalry. At Petersburg you were within the Confederate lines doing duty as a spy. First question: Is this so?"

"That would be for a rebel court-martial to prove, if I should happen to be captured."

"First question evaded. Taking advantage of the hospitality and kindness of Dr. Scoville, who had pledged his honor that you should be delivered up to the proper authorities as soon as you were able to be moved, you escaped from his custody. Second question: Is this true?"

"I was under no pledge, and was not paroled."

"Second question evaded. You are on the staff of the general of the first army corps, and you have been sent out to procure information. Third question: Is this true?"

"You have said it; not I."

"Third question evaded. By your own confession, made to me yesterday, within the Federal lines, you are a spy. You have resorted to certain Yankee tricks to escape the penalty of your misdeeds. Now — fourth question: Would it not be fair to capture you by resorting to a trick such as those you have practised?"

"It would depend on the trick."

"Fourth question evaded. You have abused the sacred rites of hospitality at the mansion of Dr. Scoville, in Virginia. Should you regard it as anything more — fifth question — than diamond cut diamond, if you should be captured in Maryland by a similar abuse of the sacred rites of hospitality?"

"That would depend on circumstances."

"Fifth question evaded. All of them evaded, as I supposed all of them would be; for a Yankee can no more avoid prevarication than he can avoid talking through his nose."

"Thank you for the handsome compliment. I cannot forget that I am speaking to a lady, and therefore I can make no answer," replied Somers, with gentle dignity, as he bowed to the tormentor.

"That is more than I expected of a Yankee," said Maud, a slight flush upon her fair cheek assuring her victim that his rebuke had been felt. "I am a lady; but before the lady, I am the Confederate woman, having a cause dearer to my heart than anything save only a woman's honor."

She spoke proudly, and her head rested with imperial grandeur on her neck as she uttered her impressive words.

"Now, Captain Somers, you understand my position, and you understand your own position," she continued. "I invited you to dine with me for a purpose. That purpose is now reached. The house is surrounded by Confederate cavalry. Captain Somers, you are a prisoner!"

## CHAPTER VI.

#### THE BOOT ON THE OTHER LEG.

LONG before the imperial, and now imperious, lady announced the conclusion of the whole matter, Somers realized that he was the victim of a conspiracy; that he had been invited to dinner in order to procure his capture. He had listened to the fallacious argument embodied in the five questions, and was prepared to refute it if occasion required. He had no difficulty in perceiving that he had got into trouble. The house was surrounded by a squad of rebel cavalry, and it would be folly to attempt to fight his way through them.

Nevertheless, Somers had coolly and decisively made up his mind not to be a prisoner. He had been invited into the house under the guise of friendship. The lady had pretended to cherish an excellent feeling, amounting almost to admiration, towards him; had treated him as a friend, and detained him until the cavalry could be sent for. The trap had been set, and he had certainly fallen into it. The circumstances were not at all like those under which he had entered the house of Dr. Scoville; he had not been invited there; he had gone in as a hunted fugitive, and the host had received and taken care of him without any pledge, expressed or implied, on his part, or that of Captain de Banyan, who accompanied him. His conscience, therefore, did not reproach him for any violation of the law of hospitality.

"You are a prisoner, Captain Somers, I repeat," said Maud — "my prisoner, if you please."

"Miss Hasbrouk, I have always cherished a feeling of admiration and regard for the ladies; but I regret, in the present instance, to be compelled to contradict you. I am not a prisoner, if you will excuse me for saying so," replied Somers, calmly.

"The house is surrounded by Confederate cavalry," added she. "It only remains for me to call them in and end this scene."

"Allow me to observe that the part which remains will be infinitely more difficult than the part already performed."

"Am I to understand, Captain Somers, that you propose to resist twenty men, who stand ready to capture you?" demanded the lady, with a triumphant smile.

"Excuse me if I evade that question also for the present. Perhaps you will still further pardon me, if, in this delicate and difficult business, I venture to ask you a few questions, which you will answer or evade, as you please."

"With great pleasure I submit to be questioned, Captain Somers," answered she, with a merry twinkle in her eyes, which told how much she still enjoyed the "situation."

"Thank you, Miss Hasbrouk. You are one of those brawling rebel women who have done so much to keep up the spirits of the chivalry in this iniquitous rebellion. You are one of the feminine Don Quixotes who have unsexed themselves in the cause of treason and slavery."

"I will not hear this, if you will, Maud. Sir!" exclaimed the major, advancing towards the bold and ungallant speaker, " your foul mouth — "

"Stand where you are, Major Riggleston!" said Somers, fiercely, as he pointed a pistol at his head. "If you stir a step, or open your mouth again, you are a dead man!"

The major seemed to be taken all aback by this decided demonstration. He had no pistol about him; and though he was a "fighting man," Somers was pretty well satisfied that he would "hold still" until it was safe for him to move. Judging from her looks, Maud seemed to be taking a slightly different view of the situation.

"Excuse my rude words, Miss Hasbrouk," continued the captain, with a gentle inclination of the head. "As this is your affair, I will thank this gentleman not to interfere. Shall I repeat what I said before?"

"It is not necessary," replied she, coldly.

"Then we will proceed. First question: Did I correctly state your position?"

"Is a woman who strengthens the hearts of those who are fighting for the right to exist—"

"First question evaded," interposed Somers. "You invited me to this house; and, by the laws of hospitality, which even the heathen respect, you were impliedly pledged to treat me as a friend, and not as a foe. Second question: Is this so?"

"Did you learn to respect the law of hospitality at Dr. Scoville's?" sneered she.

"Second question evaded. Dr. Scoville made no pledges to me, nor I to him. No person can blame me for leaving his house when I got ready. Accepting his hospitality and his kindness did not pledge me to go to a Confederate dungeon, where prisoners are systematically murdered. To proceed: By your own confession you invited me to dine in order to make me a prisoner, and take my life by having me hanged as a spy. If you sought to capture me by a trick, would it not—third question—be equally fair for me to escape by a trick?"

"But it is utterly impossible for you to escape," replied she, glancing through the window at the cavalry on the lawn.

"Third question evaded. You are a lady; and as such, under ordinary circumstances, you are entitled to be treated with the delicacy and consideration due to your sex. But as you have ceased to be a non-combatant, — which you were sorely against your will, and are now actively engaged in the war, conducting the business of capturing a prisoner, — under these circumstances, would it not be entirely fair for me to treat you as a combatant, precisely the same as though you had not unsexed yourself, and were a man?"

"You seem to have already forgotten what is due to a lady," replied she, her cheek flushed with anger.

"Fourth question evaded."

"Sir, I decline to hear any more of this coarse abuse!" exclaimed she, stamping her foot.

"Indulge me for one moment more, and I will endeavor as much as possible to avoid talking through my nose, and making pretensions as a hero of the Yankee army, or a down-east pink of chivalry."

Perhaps the imperial beauty thought that these expressions, borrowed from her own elegant discourse, were not especially refined for a lady to use; it may be that they sounded coarse on a repetition, but she made no acknowledgment to that effect.

"Your silence consents: thank you. Miss Hasbrouk, you speak with chivalrous contempt of what you are pleased to term 'Yankee tricks;' at the same time, you were thrown into spasms of laughter by the apparent success of one of your own tricks. Now, permit me to ask whether you would equally appreciate — fifth question — a trick quite as smart as your own?"

"You have insulted me long enough, sir!" replied she, haughtily. "Now, sir — "

"Fifth question evaded. I have no more to ask."

"Now, sir, I will hand you over to your masters," said she, moving a step towards the door.

"Excuse me if I take the liberty to decline being handed over to my masters," said Somers, stepping between her and the door, and now occupying a position between the lady and the discomfited major.

"Sir, what do you mean?" demanded the lady, her bosom heaving with angry emotions, as she found herself confronted by the young officer, who looked as firm and immovable as a mountain of granite.

"I mean all that I say, and much more," answered he, with an emphasis which she could not fail to understand.

"Sir, I desire to pass out at that door."

"I positively forbid your passing out at that door."

"Sir!" gasped she, almost overcome by her angry passions.

"Miss Hasbrouk!" replied he, bowing.

"You are no gentleman!"

"When I came here I regarded you as a lady, and

one of the brightest ornaments of your sex. What I think now I shall keep to myself."

"I shall go mad!"

"I hope not; though I fear you have been tending in that direction for the last hour."

"Major Riggleston!" cried she, turning to her lover, "will you stand there and permit me to be insulted in this manner?"

"Major Riggleston *will* stand there. If he moves hand or foot, or opens his mouth to speak, I will blow his brains out. He is a villain and a traitor, and of course he is a coward!"

The major winced under these strong words; but there was death in the sharp, snapping eye of the young officer, and he dared not move hand or foot, or even speak. Perhaps he thought that, as the lady had insisted on managing the affair herself, it was quite proper that she should be indulged to the end.

"I can endure this no longer!" exclaimed Maud, as she took another step towards the door for the purpose of calling in the troopers.

"Stop, Miss Hasbrouk!" said Somers, pointing a pistol at her head with his right hand, while that in his left was ready to dispose of the major.

"Is it possible that you can raise your weapon against a woman?" cried she, shrinking back from the gaping muzzle of the pistol.

The Boot on the other Leg.
Page 72.

"Let us understand each other, Miss Hasbrouk. I am not to be captured. If you attempt to leave the room, or to call in the rebel soldiers, I will shoot you, as gently and considerately as the deed can be done; but I will shoot you, as surely as you stand there and I stand here."

He cocked the pistol. She heard the click of the hammer. She stood in mortal terror of her life.

"You forget that I am a woman," said she, in tones of alarm.

"I did not forget it until you had forgotten it yourself," answered Somers. "You have abused and insulted me. Under the guise of friendship you are attempting to hand me over to death by my enemies. Did you think I would be dropped gently into the arms of the rebels, and be hung as a spy? If you insist on pursuing your plan to the end, it will be death to you or death to me. I am not quite willing to die for any rebel woman, and especially not for one who is seeking my life. It would grieve me to shoot one so fair and fascinating as Miss Hasbrouk; I should remember it with sorrow to the end of my days; but my duty to myself and my country requires the sacrifice, and I would shoot you if it broke my heart."

"Are you in earnest, Captain Somers?" asked she, still struggling under the violence of her emotions.

"Maud," said the major.

"Silence, sir!" added the captain, sternly. "Miss Hasbrouk, I am in earnest. The situation has changed. Would you like a photographer to preserve the scene for future inspection?"

"You would not kill me?"

"I would, as you would kill me."

"But the soldiers are impatient outside, and they may come in without my call," suggested she, glancing at the window, while every muscle in her frame shook with terror.

"If they do, it will cost you your life, unless they are more reasonable than you are."

"Good Heaven! You mean to murder me?"

"Not if I can help it. When I fire, it will be from a solemn sense of duty; for your cutthroats would hang me to the nearest tree if they knew as much of me as you do."

"What shall I do?" asked she, wildly, as she looked around the room.

"Now you are reasonable. Let your servant bring pen, ink, and paper."

She ordered the man who had waited on the table to bring the required articles, and Somers gave him a charge to be discreet as he left the room. In a few moments he returned with the writing materials, and laid them on the table. The negro was even more terrified than the lady, and there was no fear that he would venture upon any bold enterprise.

"Now, Major Riggleston, sit down at the table," said Somers. "You will remain where you are, Miss Hasbrouk."

"What am I to do?" asked the major.

"You will write what I dictate. Did you call this cavalry?"

"I did."

"Then you are a loyal Marylander with a vengeance, and a worthy officer of the Marlyand Home Brigade; but I will warrant there is not another such a scoundrel in the organization."

"That is a personal insult, for which —"

"Silence, sir. Who commands the cavalry outside?"

"A sergeant."

"How many men has he?"

"Twenty."

"Now write. 'Sergeant: The matter upon which I called you was all a mistake. Your services will not be required, and you will retire from the house without delay.' Sign it as you please."

Somers looked over his shoulder to satisfy himself that the major wrote what he said, and nothing else.

"It is possible we may get through this business without shooting either one of you," added the captain, as the scribe folded up the note. "Give the paper to the servant."

"Go to the front door, boy, and deliver this note to

the sergeant in command of the squad of cavalry," continued Somers.

" Yes, sar."

" Stop a moment. You are not to say a word to him."

" No, sar."

" If one of those soldiers should come into the house, it might cost your mistress her life."

" De Lo'd forbid, massa!"

" Do you understand me, boy?"

" Yes, sar. Dey shan't come in, massa, no how."

He departed on his mission. Somers still stood in the attitude for action, and Maud and the major looked as cheap and as chapfallen as though they had not another hope in the world. They waited with even more impatience than the captain for the departure of the cavalry, both of them fearing that some unfortunate accident might bring the desperate young man to the execution of his horrible threat.

The sergeant outside was, luckily, not of an inquiring mind. The clatter of horses' feet and the clanking of sabres were heard again, and the cavalry dashed down the road to more hopeful scenes.

## CHAPTER VII.

### SOUTH MOUNTAIN.

SOMERS returned the pistols to his belt as he listened to the sounds of the retreating cavalry. This action on his part seemed to afford Maud and the major an immense relief. Death no longer stared them in the face, and both of them began to grow bold again.

"Now, Major Riggleston, when you see your uncle, Dr. Scoville, again, you will have a story to tell him," said Somers.

"I shall not be likely to tell him of it."

"I think we have obtained some new ideas concerning the Yankees, to-day," added Maud, spitefully. "I had supposed their making war on women and children was merely a poetic figure; but it appears to be literally true."

"Pray, am I to regard you as a woman or a child, Miss Hasbrouk?" asked Somers; "or as both?"

"I hope I shall have the pleasure of seeing you hanged!" exclaimed she, with compressed lips.

"That's the sentiment of a woman, rather than a child," laughed Somers.

" How long before we shall be rid of your presence, Captain Somers?"

" How long will it take your servants to bring up the horse and chaise in which I saw you arrive?"

" Not ten minutes; if that will facilitate your departure, the chaise shall be brought up instantly," replied she, directing the waiter present to give the stable boys the necessary orders.

"Thank you, Miss Hasbrouk. May I trouble you also to get ready to accompany me?"

" Accompany you, sir!"

" I do not regard myself as entirely safe yet," replied the staff officer, taking one of the pistols from his belt. "Before I am out of sight, my friend the major may feel justified in calling for the cavalry again."

" They are five miles off, or will be by the time you have started," said the major.

" I think not. When I fall among people who are as sharp as you are, I always use extraordinary precautions. It is part of my purpose that you should go with us, my dear major."

" Go where?" demanded the traitor, intensely alarmed.

" I will not trouble the lady to go any farther than the farm-house where I left my horse. In regard to yourself, I shall have to insist upon your going with me to head-quarters."

"Why so?"

"You are a traitor of the blackest stamp, and it is quite proper that you should be attended to before you have done any more mischief."

"You are quite mistaken, Captain Somers. I am —"

"I will pledge myself not to prevent your escape," interposed Maud, apparently unwilling that the major should say too much.

"Excuse me, if, after what has happened, I decline to trust you."

"This is insolent, sir."

"It is open to that construction, I admit," said Somers, as he picked up the letter which the major had read with so much astonishment.

It was a blank sheet, but the direction on the outside was in a lady's handwriting, evidently Maud's. It was nothing but a "blind," to afford a reasonable pretence for the major's sudden departure. Somers put it in his pocket for future reference.

"The chaise is ready, captain," said Maud.

"So am I; but you are not."

"My hat and shawl are in the entry," she replied, sullenly.

They passed out of the house when she had robed herself for the ride. Somers assisted her into the vehicle.

"Where is the major?" asked he, turning to the spot where he had stood a moment before. Maud's reply was a silvery laugh, which was a sufficient explanation that he had taken himself off.

"So much the better," said Somers. "Good afternoon, Miss Hasbrouk," he added, as he walked rapidly up the road, in the direction of the farm-house.

She was so surprised by this sudden and unexpected change in the programme, that she could make no reply. She did not know whether the movement boded good or evil; whether the captain had gone in pursuit of the major, or to the place where he had left his horse.

Somers, when he discovered that the major had escaped him, was afraid to trust himself in the family chaise, which would too surely betray his movements to a pursuing force, if the traitor could find one in the vicinity. He decided that it would be safer for him to walk, and then he could avoid the public road if it became necessary for him to do so. Though he would have been glad to hand the treacherous scoundrel over to the military authorities for punishment as a deserter, or for giving aid and comfort to the enemy, he would have been a great encumbrance to him on the road. As events often happen for the best, he consoled himself with the belief that the traitor's escape was not the worst thing that could have occurred.

He walked rapidly till he obtained his horse. Whatever his late friends had done to secure his capture, he was not molested on the road, nor did he discover any pursuers behind him. His horse was fresh, after the long rest he had had, and Somers rode at a break-neck gait till he reached the headquarters of the general. On the way, after he had carefully arranged in his mind the information he had obtained, he could not help thinking over the exciting events of the afternoon. Major Riggleston's conduct was very strange. On the preceding day he had been a loyal soldier; now he was apparently in full sympathy with the rebels. It was a sudden change, if it was a change at all.

But the major, like a lobster, had a lady in his head, and it was quite impossible to tell what a major or a lobster would do, with a lady in his head. Somers had met the beauty at the house of Mr. Riggleston, in Frederick. They had ridden over to her home that morning in the chaise; and the best solution which he could give of the matter was, that Maud had converted him from one side to the other. As this seemed to be a satisfactory explanation of the singular conduct of the fighting man, he was satisfied with it, and gave the subject no further consideration.

His ride was not so long as it had been in the morning, for the army had advanced some miles; and at sunset Somers reported his information to the general. He also told his story about the attempt which had been made to capture him, and in the course of his narrative involved the loyal major of the Maryland Home Brigade in trouble and dishonor. The general was not a little amused at the story, and hoped other officers, who were invited to dinner by fair rebel ladies, and then entrapped, would resort to similar strategy. But the information which Somers brought was the most interesting and valuable part of the proceeds of his trip, and the general was soon busy in the study of his maps in the new light he had obtained.

The next day was Sunday; but it was not the quiet sabbath of the soul that rests the body, and renews the spirit's waning hope; it was a day of storm and battle — a day of death and destruction. Somers performed his first staff duty in the field on this occasion. During the forenoon the artillery thundered along the range of the South Mountain. The enemy was posted on the steeps, and all along the side of the mountain, on both sides of the Cumberland road, which is the direct route to the Upper Potomac. Beyond the hills were the wagon and ammunition trains of the rebels, as well as the more considerable portion of their army. The possession of this road was necessary to their safety, as well as to the success of their grand scheme of carrying on a war of invasion.

The battle was opened by the corps of General Reno, next to which in the line of march was the first army corps. During the early part of the day, the action was fought with artillery, and was an attempt to dislodge the enemy from the strong position they had taken. The slope of the mountain was rugged, consisting of irregular ledges, and the whole covered with wood, which grew out of the interstices of the rocks, and on the shelves where there was earth enough to give life to a tree. In these woods and among these rocks the rebels were located, — infantry and sharpshooters, — while their cannon were placed in such positions that they commanded all the approaches to the Gap, through which the road passed.

An attack of infantry was ordered, and the gallant fellows went forward with alacrity to execute the command. They rushed boldly up the steeps, to a stone wall behind which the main line of the enemy rested, driving the skirmishers before them. Torrents of blood flowed, and moistened the soil where hundreds of brave fellows gave up their lives; but they won the ground, and held it. The rebels fought with desperation, and their generals rallied them in vain to do what could not be done.

Partial successes and partial reverses occurred in different parts of the line until noon, when the artillery alone was actively engaged. The day was not yet won, and hundreds more were to fall on the field before the obstinate foe would yield the position.

At two o'clock in the afternoon the head of the first army corps appeared, which had been ordered forward by General McClellan to the support of Reno's hard-pressed forces. As "Fighting Joe" appeared before the lines, the utmost enthusiasm was manifested by the troops. They cheered him as though he had already saved the day. The general was examining the ground. His quick eye had already grasped the situation. He had been ordered by the general commanding to make a feint in favor of Burnside's forces; but, satisfied that an attack on the south side of the road would not be a success, he turned his attention to that portion of the rebel line at the north of the road, which had been reported upon by Captain Somers.

The general proceeded, as he always did, directly to the front. He seemed to know precisely what he was about, and to have all his force entirely in hand. Then he began to send off his orders, and the members of his staff were dashing about in every direction, till the line was formed. Batteries were posted behind the troops, and the shot and shell whizzed through the air over the soldiers' heads. The order to advance was given; the line moved up the precipitous steeps, and for half an hour the battle raged with tremendous fury.

Somers found every instant of his time occupied, as he dashed from one division to another; while shot, shell, and bullets flew through the air like hailstones. Kind Providence protected him again, as it had before, and he escaped all injury. On marched the victorious line, conquering every obstacle, and driving the rebels before them; but it was long after dark before the red field was entirely won, and the Union troops were in possession of the crests of the mountain.

"Captain Somers, you have done admirably, and fully justified my selection of you for the important and difficult position to which you have been assigned."

Somers bowed, and felt as happy as though he had commanded the successful army.

"One more task to-night, captain. You will ride to the headquarters of the army, give my compliments to General McClellan, and inform him that we have carried the position, and routed the enemy."

Somers saluted the general, and urged forward his weary horse towards Middletown. He found the commander-in-chief still in the saddle, and delivered his message. He was directed to bear the congratulations of General McClellan to the commander of the first army corps on his success, with instructions to follow up the retreating rebels, and to employ General Richardson's division, which had been sent forward to report to him, in this work, if the condition of his own troops required it.

Somers made his salute, and was riding off, thinking over what had just been said to him, as he had learned to do when sent on an errand in his childhood. He was fully absorbed in his thoughts, when a voice pronounced his name.

"Captain Somers, I am glad to see you again," said an officer, urging forward his horse to intercept him.

Somers looked at him, and was not a little surprised, in the darkness of the evening, to recognize Major Riggleston, who appeared to be one of the numerous staff of the commanding general. Perhaps it was fortunate for the messenger that he had already faithfully conned his errand, or the appearance of the traitor would have forever driven it from his mind.

"Major Riggleston!" exclaimed he, hardly able to believe the evidence of his own senses.

It was plain, after all, that he had not been fully converted to the rebel faith by the blandishments of the beautiful Maud; but he was occupying a worse and more disgraceful position, in Somers's estimation, than to have stood square up with the enemies of the country. It was most audacious in the major to hail him, after what had occurred at the mansion of the Maryland grandee, and Somers regarded him not only as a rebel, but as the stupidest rebel he had ever met.

"The same, my boy," replied the major, familiarly. "Ride on, and I will go with you a short distance, to hear the news. They say Reno was killed."

"I am sorry to say it is true," replied Somers, coldly.

"He was a brave fellow, and a splendid soldier. You must have had a warm time over there."

"Rather."

"You are tired, arn't you, old fellow? Can't you talk?"

"Not much to you," answered Somers, bluntly.

"To me? Why, what the dickens is the matter?" demanded the major, with apparent surprise.

"The matter, indeed! How does it happen that you are here?"

"Why shouldn't I be here, old boy?"

"After the affair of yesterday —"

"What affair of yesterday?"

The major had entirely lost his memory again. He had not heard a word about the adventure at the mansion of Maud's father.

## CHAPTER VIII.

### BEFORE THE GREAT BATTLE.

CAPTAIN SOMERS was as thoroughly bewildered as he would have been if the mountains around him had suddenly commenced dancing a hornpipe; or if the trees, horses, and men before him had turned bottom upwards, and the whole order of nature had been reversed. He was entirely satisfied, on reflection, that the event of the preceding afternoon had been a reality; entirely satisfied that Major Riggleston had been a party to the infamous conspiracy by which the fair Maud had sought to capture him; and the unblushing impudence of his companion in denying it passed his comprehension.

"I think you must be dreaming, Captain Somers," said the major, with a light laugh.

"Either I am, or you are; I will not pretend to say which," replied Somers, almost convinced by the words, and especially by the easy assurance of the major, that no attempt had been made to capture him; that no such person as Maud Hasbrouk had an existence.

But of course the traitor would deny his guilt; that was to be expected. It was not to be supposed that he would engage in such a nefarious scheme as that which had been exhibited at the Hasbrouk house, and then confess his participation in it. The major had actually returned to the Union lines, and had the temerity to take his place in the ranks of the defenders of the Union, even while he was, not only in heart, but openly, engaged in the service of treason and rebellion.

"Now, captain, let us be friends," continued the major; "for it really seems to me that you are disposed to provoke a quarrel with me."

"I cannot be the friend of one who is an enemy to his country," replied Somers, stiffly, and with a proper display of dignity.

"My dear fellow, I don't understand you."

"Don't understand me, Major Riggleston?" Somers began to be stern and savage.

"Upon my word I do not," protested the major, earnestly. "If you insist on picking a quarrel with me, pray tell me what it is all about."

"This is all idle talk, sir."

"You have accused me of being an enemy to my country." The major began to be slightly indignant.

"Most distinctly I accuse you of it."

"That's a grave charge."

"I am aware of it; and I speak advisedly when I

make it. If I had met General Lee himself within our lines, I should not have been more astonished than I was to see you, after what has happened."

"Will you be so kind as to tell me what has happened?" demanded the accused officer, manifesting no little excitement.

"At no distant day I shall do so before a court-martial."

"What do you mean?"

"Have you any doubt whatever in regard to my meaning?"

"Upon my word and honor as an officer and a gentleman, I have not the remotest idea what you mean."

"Major Riggleston, if the nature of my mission would permit, I would return to the headquarters of the commanding general and denounce you as a traitor."

"Captain Somers, those are words which no man can use to me with impunity," replied the major, indignantly. "I shall hold you personally responsible for them."

"I am willing to be held personally responsible for what I say," answered Somers, coolly. "If you mean violence by that remark, I shall not be off my guard."

"Captain Somers, you are a brave man. You have proved yourself to be a brave and true man," said the major, with more calmness. "I think you are too noble a fellow to vilify me without giving me an opportunity to defend myself."

"Of course you will have an opportunity to defend yourself."

"You propose to denounce me as a traitor, you say."

"I do."

"You are aware that the people of my state are divided on the great question that now disturbs the country; consequently a charge, however weak and unfounded, against me, would find plenty of believers. I have enemies. All I demand is fair play."

"You shall have it, major; for, deeply as you have injured me, or attempted to injure me, I assure you I bear no personal ill will towards you."

"Thank you for so much; but you say I have attempted to injure you. I am not conscious of any such attempt."

"Major Riggleston, this is all idle talk while you assume that position — while you pretend to be ignorant of the matter with which I charge you; and I must decline holding any further intercourse with you at present. Let me add, however, that I will not make charges until you are present to defend yourself."

"So far your conduct is honorable; if you would go a step farther, and state distinctly with what you charge me, I should be infinitely obliged to you."

"That is useless. From a gentleman I should not expect such duplicity as you exhibit in pretending to know nothing about the charge."

"I have pledged you my honor that I don't know what you mean; that I am not conscious of having given you any offence, much less done anything which can justify you in calling me a traitor."

"Do you know Miss Maud Hasbrouk?" demanded Somers.

"Of course I know her. You are perfectly aware that, though she is a rebel, she is a friend of our family."

"Good night, Major Riggleston," said Somers, as he put spurs to his steed, and dashed down the hill, leaving his companion to infer what he meant from his connection with the lady, if he needed anything to enable him to explain the nature of the charge.

The staff officer was excited and indignant that the traitor should attempt such a bold and foolish subterfuge. It was almost incredible that he should have the audacity to pretend that he did not know what the charge meant. There was no room for a doubt or a mistake. The major had positively received the blank letter; had positively gone after the rebel cavalry; had positively sustained Maud in her attempt to capture him. It was not possible, therefore, that he had done the culprit any injustice.

Thus assured that he had not wronged the major, Captain Somers again turned his attention to the message which he was to deliver to his general, and urged forward his weary horse at his best speed. He found the troops of "Fighting Joe" resting from the hard-fought action, and engaged in preparing their simple supper of coffee and "hard tack." He delivered the orders of the commanding general, and the division of Richardson was accordingly sent forward to pursue the fleeing rebels.

Early on the following morning the army advanced, and Somers found no time to think of private grievances. The general did much of his own reconnoitring on this occasion, though the members of his staff were kept constantly employed. The enemy had fallen back in disorder from South Mountain; but at ten o'clock in the forenoon the advance of the first corps came up with the position which the rebels had taken, to dispute the farther progress of the now victorious army. But the general had not at this time a sufficient force to make an attack. Antietam Creek lay between the two armies; and the bridge over it at this point was protected by the batteries which the rebels had planted to defend it.

The enemy, in two lines on the west side of the creek, were believed to consist of fifty thousand men; and the brave general impatiently awaited the arrival of the rest of the corps. It looked like an opportunity to fight a successful battle, and he was determined to cross the stream at the first practicable moment.

"General, the enemy are breaking into column and marching towards Williamsport," said Somers, as he rode up from the point at which he had been surveying the movement on the other side of the creek.

"They are on the retreat, then," replied the general.

Captain Somers and an officer of the engineers were then sent to examine the creek in search of a ford by which to transfer the troops to the other side as soon as the force of the rebels should be sufficiently reduced to justify an attack. The general chafed under the restraint which the circumstances imposed upon him; but he was too prudent to risk an attack while the advantage was so strongly against him. A ford was found near a mill, farther up the creek, and the officers reported the fact; but the arrival of the commanding general at this time prevented "Fighting Joe" from ordering an advance.

The corps remained at this place until the afternoon of the next day, when orders came to cross the creek. The troops proceeded up the stream, and went over by a bridge and by the fords which had been examined by the staff officers. The outposts of the enemy were soon discovered and driven in, and the gallant corps continued to push the force in front till it was too dark to proceed any farther, at which time the resistance was fully equal to the power of the advancing host. This was the night before the great battle of Antietam.

The weary troops lay down to rest in the cornfields where they had halted. The rebels were close by, and the pickets of the two armies were within gunshot range of each other. There was no rest yet for the general and his staff; for it was evident that a great battle was to be fought on the morrow — a battle on which the destinies of the Union depended. If the grand army of the Potomac was defeated, there would be nothing to stay the march of the invaders. The fair fields and the prosperous cities and towns of the North would then be open to them. The great heart of the nation, beating timidly as the rebel hordes advanced, sickened by previous disasters, might sink into despondency, and the bright hopes of a great people be forever crushed. It was no time for the brain of the army to slumber.

"We want information," said the general, after he had sent an aid to General McClellan to announce his intention to attack the enemy at the earliest dawn.

The commander of the first army corps always wanted information, for he never moved in the dark. His brain and his arm were twin brothers in the conflict. Somers and Barkwood volunteered to procure the information, and left the headquarters for this purpose. It was useless to attempt to penetrate the heavy picket line of the rebels in the cornfields, and they descended the hill beyond a farm-house, till they came to a ravine through which flowed a considerable volume of water.

"Here's our chance," said Somers, in a low tone.

"That's so; but you know I am a great coward, and this looks like risky business," replied Captain Barkwood.

"If you are, I think there is no need of more than one of us going through."

"O, my dear fellow, I will go with you."

"I think it would be safer for us both to separate here."

"I agree with you."

"Then I will take this ravine, and you may see what you can find farther to the north."

"Good! Now be scientific, my boy; we want to know the topography of the country as well as the position of the enemy."

"Certainly; I think I understand what is required," replied Somers, as he descended the steep bank of the ravine into the water.

The banks of the stream were of course occupied by the pickets of the two armies, and his course led him through both of them. He was just as much exposed to a shot from one as from the other. Somers was a man of experience in this business. He had earned a reputation as a scout, and had on three occasions brought in information of the utmost value to the Union commanders. Indeed, his skill in this particular branch had procured for him his promotion and his present honorable position on the staff of "Fighting Joe." He was now to undertake a fearful risk — more fearful, perhaps, than any he had before incurred; but the greater the danger, the more valuable the service rendered; and the result of to-morrow's battle might depend upon the fidelity with which he discharged his difficult duty.

He wore his long boots, and he continued to feel his way on the verge of the stream, without going in beyond his depth. The ravine was fringed with a thick growth of bushes, which shielded him from the observation of the pickets; but the slightest sound would expose him to the fire of the men. In many places the trees formed an arch over the brook, and the darkness was so dense that he could hardly distinguish an object six feet from him. He did not walk; he crept, putting his feet down as a cat does when she is on the point of pouncing on her prey.

After advancing a short distance he heard low voices on the banks above him. He was passing the first line of pickets — that of the Union army. His progress was very slow, but he succeeded in his purpose without drawing the fire of the sentinels. He was now between the two lines, and he quickened his pace a little.

While he was thus creeping through the shallow water, he discovered in the gloom a dark object before him. He paused, and ascertained that it was a human figure — a man, who had also stopped; but whether friend or enemy he could not determine.

## CHAPTER IX.

#### BETWEEN THE PICKETS.

THE man in the ravine stood stock still, and Somers stood stock still. Each had apparently discovered the other at the same moment, and each was disturbed by the same doubts in regard to the other. It was a dead lock, to all intents and purposes, for neither was willing to advance and betray himself to the other. Somers had his pistols; but a shot, if he was compelled to shoot the stranger, might call forth the fire of the pickets on both sides.

It was not a pleasant situation for either party; and they stood like black statues, each waiting for a movement on the part of the other. The only thing that Somers could do was to retire in the direction he had come; but this involved the failure of the enterprise in which he had engaged, and possibly endangered the result of the next day's battle. He was not disposed to withdraw; for if the worst came, he could shoot his opponent, and lie down under the bank of the ravine to shelter himself from the fire of the pickets. He waited a reasonable time for the dark stranger to say or do something; but as he seemed to be endowed with the patience of Job, our scout decided to take the initiative himself.

"Friend or foe?" demanded Somers, in a low tone; for he was disposed to confine the conversation to themselves.

"Friend, of course," replied the other.

"Which side do you belong to, friend?" asked Somers, deeming the answer rather indefinite.

"To the Union side, of course," replied the stranger, with refreshing promptness.

There was no non-committal about him, as might have been expected, half way between the lines of the two armies, and Somers was pretty well satisfied that he was what he claimed to be.

"Where are you going?"

"That's rather a delicate question, Captain Somers, my dear fellow," responded the stranger. "You are evidently at your old tricks, captain."

"Who are you?" demanded Somers, not a little surprised and disconcerted at being recognized in his present situation.

"Don't you know me?" added the stranger, advancing cautiously towards the captain.

"I haven't that pleasure."

"Yes, you have; though it is rather dark here for a

man to make out even his best friend. I am Major Riggleston."

"Are you, indeed?" exclaimed Somers, taken all aback by the announcement.

He would rather have met Stonewall Jackson under the circumstances. He could not imagine what the major could possibly be doing in such a place at such an hour of the night, unless he was crawling into the rebel lines, to take a part with the foe in the expected battle. He was tempted to shoot him on the spot, and thus, while he removed an obstacle in his own path, rid the country of a traitor and a dangerous enemy; but Somers never had the nerve to do anything that looked like deliberate murder.

"Major Riggleston, you are a mystery to me," said he.

"So I am to all who know me," replied the major. "Come, captain, let us sit down and talk over the matter. If we speak low, the pickets will not hear us. You are a man after my own heart, and I desire to have you understand me better."

"I think I understand you very well."

"No, you don't; you just now said I was a mystery to you," chuckled the major.

"I mean that I understand your objects — that you are a traitor to your cause and country."

"My dear captain, you never made a greater blunder in your life."

"I don't see it."

"You shall see it, in the course of ten minutes, if you will hear me."

"It is useless for me to hear you. I shall not believe a word you say, after what passed between us yesterday."

"What was that?"

"Didn't you deny all knowledge of the affair at the Hasbrouk house."

"'Pon my word I did not."

"You did not?"

"No."

"You have the worst memory of any man in Maryland."

"That may be."

"Did you, when we met last evening—"

"We didn't meet last evening," interposed the major.

"You have a most astonishing memory. I denounced you as a traitor."

"It wasn't kind of you to do that," laughed Riggleston.

"Perhaps not; but it was true. You didn't know what I meant; you hadn't the least knowledge of the affair at the Hasbrouk house?"

"Of course not, over there!"

The major took off his cap and scratched his head. The act seemed suddenly to vivify his memory.

"O, I do remember meeting you last night," said he.

"Very good; I have some hope of you, at last. Now, can you recall the event to which I alluded?"

"Perfectly."

"That you, in connection with Miss Hasbrouk, attempted to procure my capture by the rebels?"

"I acknowledge the soft impeachment; but the affair is susceptible of a different construction from that you put on it."

"I think not."

"Upon my word it is, my dear fellow. I intend to prove it, and I am sure you will agree with me."

"First, will you explain to me how you happen to be in this ravine, at this hour of the night, and when we are on the eve of a great battle?" asked Somers.

"I could explain it to your undoubted satisfaction, my dear captain; but you must excuse me for the present."

"I can't excuse you; and we may as well fight it out now as at any other time. You are a rebel, and I am a Union man. In the words of Mr. Seward, there is an irrepressible conflict between us. You have caught me, and I have caught you. I don't propose to shirk the responsibility of my position; but I suppose one of us must die, or be severely wounded, to insure the safety of the other."

Somers cocked his pistol. He had already made up his mind in regard to the presence of Major Riggleston at this place. His theory was, that the fellow was a scout, like himself, if he was not a professional spy; that at the time they happened to meet, the major was passing over from the Union to the rebel lines, for the purpose of imparting to Stonewall Jackson, who was understood to be in command of the Confederate left wing, information in regard to the strength and position of General McClellan's forces.

"For Heaven's sake, Captain Somers, don't fire upon me!" exclaimed the major, as he heard the click of the pistol.

There could be no doubt of the sincerity of the fellow in the use of these words. Somers judged, from what he had seen of him, that he was one of those persons who were born to creep, but by some blunder had walked upright, and thus deceived the world in regard to their true character. Though he called himself a fighting man, he was a cringing coward, as Somers had twice before had occasion to observe.

"I have no wish to shoot you, Major Riggleston. I would much rather be spared that pain," said Somers. "You have crossed my path, and you interfere with my plans."

"You are mistaken again. I propose to explain everything, and then we shall understand each other perfectly. You are a scout, and so am I. You are obtaining information; so am I. You are a true Union man; so am I."

"I don't believe you."

"Here is my pass; that will convince you."

"I can't see to read it."

"I will light a match. It will not be seen in this hole."

The major handed him a paper, and struck a match against the inside of his cap.

"Now read quick."

Somers read: "The bearer, Major Riggleston, of the —nd Maryland Home Brigade, is a true and loyal man, and as such entitled to receive protection and assistance from all officers and soldiers of the United States." The document was duly signed and countersigned by high and proper authority, and the date was within the current month and year. The captain was astonished beyond measure, for he had no doubt of the correctness of this safe-conduct. It knocked his little theory all to pieces, and he was forced, for the first time, to believe that he had misjudged the major.

"Where are you bound now?" asked he.

"Just where you are."

"Do you carry this paper with you?"

"Always; my life would not be safe a moment without it."

"I should say your life would not be safe with it, if it were discovered upon you within the rebel lines."

"There is no danger on that score. I take good care of it. Are you satisfied, Captain Somers?"

"I am satisfied with the paper; but I think your employers do not expect you to entrap Union officers, as you attempted to do at the Hasbrouk house."

"My dear fellow, I did not intend to do anything of the kind."

"You were certainly a party to the transaction."

"Apparently I was; really I was not. Now that you understand the first part of the story, I will explain the second. You know Miss Hasbrouk?"

"Certainly I know her."

"She is a beautiful girl — isn't she?"

"There can be no doubt on that point; but I suppose you will tell me next that she is not a rebel, and that she was working for the United States government when she got up that little conspiracy, and attempted to have me hung."

"On the contrary, she is a rebel. Jeff Davis himself is not a more thorough-going rebel, and she was fully in earnest when she attempted to make you a prisoner."

"But you assisted her."

"Apparently only; if you had been handed over to the cavalry, as I supposed you would be, it would have been my privilege, as it would have been my duty, to get you out of the scrape, which I could very easily have done. Maud regards me as a rebel."

Somers could not help thinking that she was more than half right, but he was prudent enough not to give voice to his thought on this subject.

"You helped her through with the whole thing."

"Undoubtedly I did, but with the intention that you should not suffer. You are aware that she planned the scheme herself; I was dragged into it, and I could not resist without impairing her confidence in me."

"You seem to value very highly the confidence of a rebel woman."

"For the sake of my suffering country I do. Maud is a beautiful girl; you acknowledge that. Well, the rebel officers think so, too," added the major, pausing as if to give his companion an opportunity to comment on this remarkable partiality; or perhaps to note the bearing of the fact on their intimate relations.

"They are gentlemen of taste," was all the comment Somers deemed it necessary to make.

"Maud is an enterprising woman. She takes a deep interest in all army movements, and worms out of the rebel officers much valuable information, which I in turn worm out of her; for I need hardly tell you that the relations between Maud and myself are of the pleasantest character."

"Lovers?" added Somers.

"Yes, if you please."

"It seems to me that is using a very sacred relation for a very vicious purpose," replied the captain, whose fine sentiment was not a little shocked at the thought of lovers mutually deceiving each other.

"We work for our country, Captain Somers."

"Go on, major."

"Don't you understand it all now?"

"I think I do; at least, enough of it to comprehend your position."

Somers, in spite of himself, was not entirely satisfied; certainly not with the character of the man, if he was with the genuineness of his mission.

"Which way were you going when I met you?" asked he.

"The same way that you were," replied the major, with some hesitation. "If you please, we will go on together. You report to one general, and I to another; but the substance of our information must be the same. We will go on together, and return together."

"I don't know about that."

"I am entirely safe within the rebel lines. If we have passed the Yankee pickets, we have nothing more to fear."

The *Yankee* pickets! This was not the form of expression usually adopted by loyal men; and it was the second time he had detected his interesting companion in using it. It seemed to be habitual with him; but perhaps it was because he had spent so much of his time within the rebel lines, pursuing the duties of his calling.

"I think we had better keep within the ravine."

"Very well; but I have a rebel safe-conduct."

"Would you let me see them both, if you please."

"Certainly, if you desire it," replied the major, but with evident reluctance.

He produced them both, with the remark that it was not necessary to read the true one again; but Somers wished it, and he yielded. The major lighted a match, and the captain read both the documents. As he finished the match went out, and they were in total darkness again.

"What's that?" said Somers, suddenly springing to his feet, with the papers in his hand.

It was a shot from the pickets; but there had been one every ten minutes since they sat down.

## CHAPTER X.

### MAJOR RIGGLESTON.

SOMERS had thrust the papers into his pocket, pretending to fear a sudden onslaught of the pickets; but the alarm passed without any consequences, serious or otherwise.

"We are perfectly safe, captain," said Major Riggleston. "I believe you did not give me back my papers."

"Here they are," replied he, handing him the blank letter which had played so important a part in the attempt to capture him at the Hasbrouk house, and which he had put in his pocket at the time. "We are losing the whole night, and we had better move on. I am satisfied with the prospect, but I would rather not expose myself to the rebel pickets."

"As you please; we can go through this place without being seen or heard. But I am well known all through the rebel army, and I shall not be molested when I give my name."

"Then you will be a useful friend to me."

"That's what I have been trying to prove to you.

Perhaps I ought to say that I actually hold a commission in the Confederate cavalry, which enables me to stand square before the rebels while I give information to our own people. You understand me."

"Perfectly."

"I have told you what no other living man knows; for even the high authority that employs me has no conception of the means by which I procure my information. I have trusted you, because you are a man after my own heart. What you did in Virginia endears you to me. We are kindred spirits, and it is proper that we should understand each other."

Somers hoped they were not kindred spirits; for if the major was what he claimed to be, there could be but little sympathy between them. He was a coward and a brag; and he told more lies than even his dangerous profession required. He used the sacred relations of life for his own purposes. But Somers was not satisfied, as we have before suggested. The major had a safe-conduct from the authorities on both sides; and whatever weight he had given to the loyal one was neutralized by the production of the other. It was possible that he had procured it for the purpose of doing Union work; but one pass nullified the other; and the captain was still in doubt as to which side his versatile companion actually belonged — so much in doubt that he was fully determined not to run any risks.

Major Riggleston led the way up the ravine, both of them creeping and crawling at a snail's pace, so as not to attract the attention of the pickets on the bank above them. Somers would not have been very much surprised if the "kindred spirit" before him had summoned the soldiers to make him a prisoner; but he stood prepared for such an emergency. His pistol was ready for immediate use; and if a scene occurred, he trusted to the darkness of the night and the friendly shelter of the ravine to promote his escape.

Apparently the highly respectable scout in his company had no intention of betraying him, for they passed in safety through the line of rebel pickets, and emerged from the ravine into a grove of oaks. If the major had set a trap to make him a prisoner, or had resorted to a scheme to save himself from a personal encounter in the lonely gorge, there was no longer any need that he should keep up his pretensions, for the camp fires of the rebels were to be seen in every direction. Only a few rods from the spot where they stood there was a body of cavalry bivouacking on the ground.

Somers was a prey to the most painful doubts. Uppermost in his mind was the wish to discharge with fidelity the difficult and dangerous task which had been imposed upon him; and if Major Riggleston was what he claimed, he would be an invaluable assistant to him. His two passes, one from each party in the great strife, proved nothing for or against him. It was utterly impossible, therefore, to reach a satisfactory conclusion in regard to his companion. But it was not prudent to place himself in a situation where he could be easily captured. All he could do was to permit affairs to take their own course until some further developments should enable him to act intelligently. As they were now actually within the rebel lines, the conclusion of the whole matter must soon be reached.

"This is rather dangerous business," said the major, as they stepped from the bank into the oak grove.

"We must proceed with the utmost caution," replied Somers, nervously, as he gazed earnestly at his associate, to obtain, if he could, any clew to his purpose.

"If you confide in me, Captain Somers, you will be safe, unless some stupid sentinel takes it into his head to fire upon us, which is really the only danger we incur."

"I think we had better avoid these camps and squads of soldiers as much as possible. Do you know where the main line of Jackson's army is?"

"Certainly I do; I will show it to you in due time."

"Is he fortified?"

"You shall see in a short time."

"How many men has he?"

"About seventy thousand."

Somers knew better than this; and the answer sounded very much like a Confederate reply to a Union question.

"Now follow me," said the major, "and whatever happens, don't be alarmed."

Riggleston led the way through the grove; but they had advanced only a few paces before they were challenged by a rebel soldier. The major replied to the demand with easy self-possession, informing the soldier who he was. It was all right, and they were permitted to proceed on their way.

"You see it is all right, captain," said the major, as they entered the open field beyond the grove.

"They know you very well."

"Of course they do."

"If you know all about the situation and the force of the rebels, what is the use of going any farther?"

"I don't know," replied the major, rather confused at the question. "But, Somers, you wear your staff uniform."

"I do."

"That's a mistake. It will expose yourself and me," he added, with some appearance of alarm. "If I had seen what you had on before, I should not have dared to come with you."

"I don't intend to show myself to these people."

"But we were challenged only a moment since; and if the soldiers had noticed your uniform, they would have detained you."

"If I had been alone, I should not have exposed myself to their gaze."

"It's a mistake, and we must correct it."

"Half the rebel officers wear Union colors. They rob our people of their coats, and don't scruple to wear them."

"But a staff uniform!"

"I think we had better separate here; I will take care of myself, and you can pursue your investigations in your own way."

"You would be taken in less than half an hour. There is a house over here, where I can get you a farmer's frock, or something of that kind."

"Then, if taken, I am an officer in disguise; and it would go hard with me."

"I think it would any way."

"Perhaps it would."

"You are pretty well known by reputation. You had better change your name."

"Perhaps I will, if I have to give my name."

"Who goes there?" demanded a squad of men, as they were on the point of crossing a rough farm-road.

"Friends," replied the major.

"Who are you?"

"Major Riggleston."

"We have just caught a Yankee spy — a fellow crawling into our lines," replied one of the men.

There were four of them; they had a prisoner whom they were conducting up the road towards the main body of Jackson's division.

"Where did you get him?"

"Up in the cornfield beyond. He was crawling on his hands and knees between the rows, and had got almost through when we found him. We shall do some hanging in the morning. What shall we do with him, major?"

Somers looked with interest and sympathy at the poor fellow thus entrapped; but the major was a Union man, and of course he would save him from his fate the moment he could consistently with the duty of keeping up appearances.

"Take him up to this house," said the major, pointing in the direction he was leading Somers.

The men obeyed. Their dangling sabres indicated that they belonged to the cavalry; and the obedience they rendered to Major Riggleston further indicated that they belonged to his battalion.

"Why should these men obey you?" asked Somers, wishing to settle this point.

"They are my men. I told you I held a commission in the cavalry — for the good cause, you know."

"I understand."

"By the way, captain, have you seen Miss Hasbrouk since we met last?"

"I have not."

"She follows the army."

"Which army?"

"The rebel army, of course."

"What for?"

"Because she likes it, I suppose. She is very useful as a nurse, they say. Of course I don't discourage her; for I make her serviceable to the good cause, you know."

The farm-house was now in sight, and there was a light in one of the front rooms. Without the ceremony of knocking, the major opened the door and entered, ordering the four cavalrymen to follow him with their prisoner.

"Come in," said he.

"Who is in this house?" demanded Somers, shrinking from the light which he saw within.

"Only women, with a few wounded men. I want to see this prisoner, and find a good excuse for letting him go," replied the major, in a whisper.

Somers entered the house, where the prisoner had already been conducted. To his surprise and chagrin he discovered that the unfortunate was Captain Barkwood; but the major did not seem to recognize his companion in the skirmish on the road and at the house of Mr. Riggleston in Frederick.

"Two of you hold your prisoner," said the major to the soldiers, as they entered the small room.

"Now, Captain Somers," he added, when Captain Barkwood had been placed in a corner with two men holding him, "allow me to add, that we have carried this farce quite far enough, and that you are also a prisoner."

At this moment, to the astonishment of Somers, Maud Hasbrouk entered the room to learn the cause of the commotion, — for it appeared afterwards that she was here nursing a couple of officers who had been wounded at South Mountain.

"Why, major, I did not expect to see you at this early hour of the night," said she.

"I have brought up one of your friends," added he, laughing, as he pointed at Somers.

"Captain Somers!" exclaimed she, as a smile of triumph lighted up the features of the beauty. "This is an unexpected pleasure. I hope you are quite well, Captain Somers."

"As well as usual, I thank you," replied he.

We need not add that he was bewildered by the new situation, and roundly condemned his own folly in permitting himself to be led into such a trap. It was quite evident that the treacherous major had brought him to this house for the purpose of permitting Miss Maud to enjoy the triumph. He was determined not to afford her much satisfaction. It might prove to be a hanging affair to him, and he felt himself warranted in resorting to the most desperate remedies. It was better to die by a bullet or a sabre cut than perish by the rope.

"I have been entertaining our friend the captain for

the last hour with an account of my services to the Yankees, all of which he has swallowed as a fish does a worm, without seeing the hook within. He came here like a lamb; and as you had some sparring with him on a former occasion, when he rather got the better of you, I thought you would like to see him before I send him and the other enterprising gentleman to the rear."

"I am delighted to see him. And the other gentleman is Captain Barkwood. He belongs to the regulars."

"I never saw him before," replied the major.

Somers thought he had another attack of bad memory; but the situation was too exciting to permit him to dwell on minor discrepancies. When the major called him a prisoner, Somers had quietly fallen back into the corner of the room behind the door by which he had entered. Barkwood had been thrust back into another corner at his left, while Maud and the major stood diagonally opposite to him, and near the door by which she had entered from the chamber of her patients. The two cavalrymen not employed were standing half way between Somers and Barkwood.

"I'm sure I am delighted to see you, Captain Somers," laughed Maud. "I came over here to take care of two sick friends, and expected nothing but a melancholy time. Your presence fills me with satisfaction."

"I am greatly obliged to you, and thankful that I am

able to do something more towards discharging the debt of gratitude I owe to you for your kindness on a former occasion. You are fond of situations, and I am again the central figure in one," answered Somers, without any apparent appreciation of the difficulty and danger of his position. "Would you like to ask me any questions?"

"I cannot stop to question you now; my patients need my care. You would evade them if I did; besides, this is Major Riggleston's affair, not mine," replied she, with a mocking laugh.

"And I will take care that this affair don't go wrong," said the major. "Soldiers, secure your prisoners."

The two men moved towards Somers in the corner.

## CHAPTER XI.

#### SHOT IN THE HEAD.

THE critical moment, when everything depended upon the wisdom and energy of the next move, had arrived. As Major Riggleston issued his order, Somers raised one of his pistols, and, taking hasty but careful aim at his treacherous companion, fired. While her accepted suitor was uttering his mandate, Maud, as if fearing a repetition of the uncomfortable proceeding at the Hasbrouk house, retreated into the apartment occupied by her patients. The ball struck the major in the head, and he fell, with a shock that caused the rude structure to tremble.

A half-suppressed shriek from the sick room assured those in the front apartment that Maud was aware active proceedings had commenced, though she could not have known who was the first victim in the encounter. The two soldiers, who had been ordered to arrest the staff officer, were bold enough to move upon their intended victim; but they only rushed upon the barrel of a revolver, pointed by the hand of one skilled in the business, and collected enough to do his work carefully and effectively.

Again Somers fired, and the foremost of the two soldiers fell dead upon the floor. He fired a third time, and the other soldier shrank back with the ball in his right shoulder. The two men in charge of Captain Barkwood had been too often in the midst of death and carnage to be appalled by these exciting events.

"Hold this man!" exclaimed the more decided of the two, "and I will make short work of that fellow."

"Shoot him," replied the other. "Do it quick."

He attempted to do it quick; too quick, for he missed his mark. He fired again, but the smoke impaired his aim. At this moment Captain Barkwood, conscious that the time for a demonstration in favor of his friend had come, with a sharp, nervous movement, freed himself from the grasp of the rebel in charge of him, and struck him a tremendous blow in the temple with his bare fist, which felled him to the floor. Not satisfied with this deed, he sprang upon the other soldier, who was in the act of firing upon Somers for the third time. Grasping him by the shoulders with both hands, he brought his knee violently into the small of his back, and thus threw him down. Seizing his pistol, he struck him a heavy blow on the head with the weapon.

"I surrender," said the wounded man, — who was the

only one of the four in condition to speak, — as Somers moved towards him.

The young captain took the sabre from his belt, and opening the window, tossed it out. All active opposition had been conquered, but two of the men were only stunned, and in a short time they would probably be able to speak and act for themselves.

"Captain Somers, I would hug you if I had time," said Barkwood. "What shall we do next?"

"I hardly know," replied Somers. "If we leave the house, we may fall into the hands of the first squad of soldiers we meet. Besides, we have not done our work yet. We must first look after the lady."

Somers, stepping over the body of Major Riggleston, which lay near the door, entered the apartment occupied by the wounded officers. There was no light there, and he returned to bring that in the front room. He found Maud standing in the middle of the room, apparently paralyzed with terror.

"Miss Hasbrouk, here is another officer who needs your care, if he is not already past it."

"What do you mean?" asked she, in husky tones.

"Major Riggleston has fallen."

She uttered a faint scream. She was so enfeebled by terror that she seemed not to have the strength to do anything. She was more at talking than she was at acting.

"What shall I do?" asked she.

"Come and see," replied he.

She timidly followed him into the adjoining room, and gazed with fear and trembling upon the form of the major.

"Is he — is he — dead?" gasped she.

"I don't know," replied Somers, stooping down, and glancing at the wound on the major's head. "No, he is not dead, and probably will not die with that wound."

"What shall I do? Will you call a surgeon?"

"I think not."

"We have no time to spare, Captain Somers," interposed the regular, with a smile at the simple question of the frightened Maud.

"We will make our escape. We will go by the grove to the north of the house — to the *north*," said Somers, with peculiar emphasis.

"To the north," repeated Barkwood, with the same emphasis, though he did not understand the strategy of his companion.

"We need not hurry; the more haste, the less speed in the business," replied Somers, as he bent over the prostrate form of the major again.

This time he took from his body the large, loose coat which the treacherous rebel had worn, and picked up the felt hat, adorned with a black feather, which had dropped from his head.

"He is killed," said Maud, who was beginning to recover her self-possession.

"Perhaps he is; but that is his fault, not mine," replied Somers, as he led the way out of the door, followed by the regular. "If either of you attempt to follow us, or leave the house within half an hour, it will cost you your lives," he added, addressing Maud and the wounded soldier.

"May I not send for a surgeon?" asked she, with a meekness which ill comported with her former imperious manner.

"No."

"But the major will die."

"I can't help it."

"I will not say anything about you, if you will allow me to send for assistance."

"Half an hour will make no difference to him," answered Somers, as he left the house. "Come with me," added he to the regular, when they reached the open air.

He led the way to the rear of the house, where there were a number of sheds, and other out-buildings, used for various farm purposes. One of these he entered, followed by the regular, who seemed to repose unlimited confidence in the tact and ability of his young companion.

"What next, Somers?" asked Barkwood, in a whisper.

"Nothing just yet. There will be a tremendous row round here in the course of ten minutes, or at most half an hour. All we want just now is a snug place to lie by in until the tempest blows over."

"But you are not going to stop here — are you?" demanded the regular, in a tone which sufficiently expressed his astonishment at such a policy.

"This is the best place in the world for us. I am not a strategist, as you are, captain; but I have a fixed principle for use in cases of this kind, and that is, to stow myself away in a place where they are least likely to look for me."

"Very good; but where is that place?"

"Here, in this house."

"That's cool."

"But it is the best logic in the world. I don't want to influence you in your movements, Captain Barkwood; but I don't intend to return without the information which I came out to procure. If you want to return to the camp, I will tell you how you can manage, though I think you had better remain with me."

"I am entirely of your opinion," whispered the regular, with a suppressed chuckle. "You are an old head at this business, and I am as green at it as a two months baby."

"As you please, captain. For my own part, I feel tolerably safe now. I was a fool to trust that Riggleston."

"He is an infernal villain."

"Hush!" said Somers, finding his companion was becoming a little too emphatic for safety. "I must find a place to stow you away."

In the back room of the house, which was only a shed attached to the rear of the building, Somers found a large closet, which seemed to be a kind of lumber room. In this he bestowed his companion, and rolled a large chopping-block up before the door. While he was engaged in this operation, the door leading from the kitchen into the shed opened, and an old black woman rushed out, apparently deeply moved by some circumstance which Somers had no difficulty in understanding. She had a light in her hand, which at once revealed to her the presence of a stranger upon her own peculiar territory.

"De Lo'd!" exclaimed she, starting back with alarm.

"Silence, aunty! Don't speak again," said Somers, in a low tone.

"Gracious! Dat's Massa Riggleston!" added she, shrinking back.

The scout had put on the great coat and feathered hat of the major, which seemed to explain the terror of the woman.

"Where are you going, aunty?"

"For de doctor," said she; "but if you be de ghost

ob Massa Riggleston, 'taint no use for de doctor, for de major must be dead."

"No matter what I am, aunty. Come with me."

"De Lo'd sabe us!"

"If you behave yourself, and don't make a noise, I will not hurt you," said he, as he led the way out of the shed.

"Where be I gwine, massa?"

"No matter; keep still."

A few steps from the door was a small tool-house, which Somers opened, and ordered the woman to go in. She tremblingly obeyed, and he closed the door upon her, with an injunction to keep entirely silent, which she seemed disposed to obey. Fastening the door upon her, he returned to the house, satisfied that she would not further interfere with his plans.

The black woman had left the kitchen door open, and Somers walked in, with the light in his hand. There was a fire in the stove, on which there were several dishes of gruel, and other articles necessary for the sick room. It was evident that the farmer and his family had been turned out of the house, for no other persons appeared to disturb his operations. His long, heavy boots were not favorable to stealthy movements, and he retired to the back room to remove them. After satisfying himself, by a further examination, in regard to the structure of the house, and the position of the doors and windows, he extinguished the light, and passed from the kitchen to the front entry.

The door connecting with the front room, where the exciting events of the evening had occurred, was open. Maud, in the deepest distress, was talking to the wounded soldier. He was unable or unwilling to do anything, and Maud depended upon the black woman for aid. Somers concealed himself under the stairs, and waited for further developments.

He was not compelled to wait long; for presently he heard footsteps, which indicated the arrival of at least half a dozen persons.

" It is hardly time for the return of Major Riggleston," said one of them.

" We are rather early; but when he comes, he will bring us the fullest intelligence," added another, as they entered the front room.

Then there was a commotion, which was produced by the discovery of what had taken place in the apartment. There was nothing but a board partition between Somers and the interior of the room, and he could distinctly hear everything that was said. Maud told, in few words, what had happened in the room; that Major Riggleston had been shot in the head in his attempt to capture two prisoners, and that the men who had done the foul deed had escaped. From what was said it was evident that one of the officers was a person high in command — a general of division, if not Stonewall Jackson himself. The others called him simply "general," and Somers could not determine who he was. The officers with him were probably members of his staff.

The general immediately despatched one of his officers to institute a strict search for the spies who had done this terrible work. He regretted that it had not been discovered before; for the miscreants, as he called them, in the most complimentary terms, were probably a good distance from the house by this time.

"I know which way they went, general," said Maud, eagerly. "They went to the north of the house."

"To the north, general," added the wounded soldier; for both of them had carefully treasured up this information, dropped hastily from the mouths of the scouts, for future use, as Somers intended they should.

"Very well; pursue them towards the north, colonel," resumed the general. "But don't say a word about what has happened in this house till morning. It will help us in the search."

The speaker proceeded to give very careful directions for the pursuit and the search, to all of which Somers listened with the deepest interest. The colonel who had been charged with the duty, departed.

"What do you think of him, doctor?" asked Maud, revealing to the listener the fact that one of the officers was a surgeon.

She was sad and depressed, and asked the question with trembling tones, which betrayed her solicitude for the wounded major.

"I don't think he is very badly wounded. The ball has passed through his head; but worse cases than this have occurred, and the patients are alive and well to-day," replied the surgeon.

The wounded man was taken up and borne to a bed in the chamber with Maud's other patients; after which the soldiers received some attention.

## CHAPTER XII.

### THE COUNCIL OF OFFICERS.

SOMERS heard all that was said in the front room, and judged from that, and the sounds which reached him, what was taking place there. The two men who were stunned came to their senses, after a while, and they were sent off with the dead and the wounded ones; for it appeared that the general wanted the apartment for a consultation with his officers. It was expected that Major Riggleston would be present at this place with fresh information from the Yankee lines; and the listener congratulated himself that he had been able to disappoint them in this respect.

The major had chosen the ravine for his passage through the pickets, and it was now evident that he intended to resume his work as soon as he had disposed of his prisoner. The fellow was armed with a pass, and, Somers well knew, was regarded in the loyal lines as a major of the —nd Maryland Home Brigade, and could therefore go where he pleased, even into the very councils of the general commanding the army of the Potomac.

Somers believed he had made a great discovery. The rebels always knew precisely when and where the army of the Potomac were going to move. When McClellan had actually made up his mind to attack the forces fortified at Manassas, they suddenly decamped. All his movements for months were mysteriously communicated to the enemy, even before the general officers of the loyal army were informed in regard to them. People wondered, the press commented severely, and the government was perplexed.

Captain Somers thought he understood all about it now, and believed that he had laid out the man who had done all this mischief. Much as we admire the captain, our hero, we are compelled to say that he was mistaken. He had really made no such discovery, and had achieved no such tremendous result as the killing of the one who had done this immense injury to the loyal cause, as future pages in our history will show. But he believed Major Riggleston, whom he had seen in the staff of the general commanding, was the man who had conveyed all this information; he believed he had made this great discovery, accomplished this big thing; and he took courage accordingly.

Major Riggleston was not there to speak of what the Yankees had done, and what they intended to do; but for all this, the consultation of officers proceeded. Somers heard them discuss their own position and that of the enemy; he heard them suggest all manner of possibilities and probabilities, and how to meet them; but they did not speak so definitely as he wished they would. They alluded to a line of field-works, which the listener was unable to locate.

Somers was coiled up behind a chest of drawers, and did not concern himself at all about his personal safety. He was too deeply interested in the labors of the council to think of himself. He had a tolerably good idea of the rebel plans, and wondered whether the man who was called "general" was really Stonewall Jackson. He could not reach a satisfactory conclusion on this point, but he was strongly in favor of the supposition.

"It is one o'clock, and we must get a little sleep," said the mysterious general, as Somers heard the rattling of chairs when they rose from the table.

"Some of us will probably make a long sleep of it to-morrow," added one of the officers.

"Don't trifle with a matter so serious," continued the general, solemnly. "Ah, here is the colonel," he added, as the door opened, and two or three persons entered the house. "What news do you bring? Have you captured those Yankees?"

"I have neither captured them nor heard a word of them. Not a soul within our lines knows anything about them," replied the colonel, in tones of disgust and mortification.

"That's singular. Our sentinels are sleepy; they must be stirred up. The miscreants had not been gone from this house more than twenty minutes when we arrived, according to the statement of the lady."

"Nothing was ever more thoroughly done than the search we made; but I am positive they have got through."

"Perhaps not," suggested the general.

"I have searched every house, grove, and clump of trees; every hole, ditch, and cornfield within two miles of this spot. I am satisfied, but I believe there are traitors within our camp. They could not have got through without help from our side of the line."

"We will look into that matter at the first opportunity," replied the general, with a long gape.

They left the house in a body, and all was silent within, except the step of Maud Hasbrouk, as she attended to the wants of the sufferers in her care. Somers had done all he could do in this place, and he was satisfied that the search for himself and Captain Barkwood had been abandoned. He crawled out of the corner in which he had been coiled away for over two hours, intent upon the great duty which was still in a measure unperformed. He had some doubts whether his friend in the closet had been patient under the long delay; and he was in haste to relieve him from the suspense and discomfort of his situation.

There was no one in the house but Maud and her three patients. There was, therefore, nothing to fear, and he crept towards the door leading from the entry into the kitchen. He softly opened it, and was stealthily making his way towards the shed, when the door of the front room was thrown wide open, and Maud, apparently in a great hurry, stepped into the kitchen. She had a bowl in her hand, and was intent upon the object which had brought her there, so that she did not at first see Somers, who stood in the middle of the floor.

When she discovered him she screamed, and started back in astonishment and terror, dropping the dish; but she still held the light which she had brought from the sick room. Somers regarded the meeting as a very unfortunate occurrence, and wished he had been prudent enough to go out at the front door; but it was too late to indulge in vain regrets, and the situation was sufficiently perilous to induce him to resort at once to decisive measures, for the tongue of the woman was hardly less dangerous than a squad of rebel cavalry.

"Who are you?" asked the lady, when she had recovered herself sufficiently to speak.

"It matters not who I am," replied Somers, disguising his voice as much as he could.

"Captain Somers!" exclaimed she, shrinking back still farther.

"I am sorry, for your sake, that you have recognized

me," replied he, dropping the collar of his coat, which he had drawn up over his face. "Miss Hasbrouk, your discovery endangers my life; I am compelled either to shoot you, or —"

"To shoot me!" exclaimed she, with horror.

"What is the matter, Maud?" said a voice from the front room, which was followed by the appearance of Major Riggleston, whose head was tied up with bandages, as the surgeon had dressed it.

"It is Captain Somers," said she, in trembling tones.

"It seems that I did not fully do my work," added Somers, taking a pistol from his belt.

"Don't fire, Somers, don't," said the major, in tones so feeble and piteous that Somers could not help being moved by them. "You have nearly killed me now, and you ought to be satisfied."

"It is your life or mine, Major Riggleston, and I have no time to argue the matter. In five minutes more you will have the whole Confederate army at my heels. I run no risks with a villain like you," replied Somers.

"Don't fire!" begged Maud; "I will do anything you desire, if you will spare me."

It was something to see a brawling rebel woman, the most pestilent and inveterate enemy the government had in the contest, in a pleading posture. It was something to expose the ridiculous pretensions of one of that army of female rebels, fiercer and more vindictive than the men, and to demonstrate that she had none of the courage of which she had boasted. Maud regretted that her sex compelled her to be a non-combatant; it was doubtful whether she would ever again regret it.

"I wish not to take the life of either of you; but my own safety compels me to use strong measures," said Somers, as he cocked his pistol.

"For mercy's sake, don't fire!" gasped Maud.

"Don't kill me, Somers; I will pledge you my word and honor not to expose you," added the major.

"What are your word and honor good for, after what has happened this night?" sneered Somers.

"I will give you all the information you require, if you will spare my life."

"That would not save my life."

"I will give you the countersign."

"That's something towards it."

The wretch gave him the word, and while he received it, he despised the major more than ever before. He was now a traitor to both sides; but all this, and more, would *he* give in exchange for his life. Somers then questioned him in regard to the position of various bodies of rebel troops, and the miscreant answered him promptly, and, as it was afterwards shown, correctly.

"You know me now, Major Riggleston and Miss Hasbrouk; and you must understand that I go about with my life in my hand. I am not to be trifled with. I will not take your life yet."

"I will swear never to reveal your presence to a living soul," exclaimed the major.

"You need not; you have given me better security than your oath that you will not expose me. If I am taken, I shall be taken with the countersign in my keeping. I had it from you. If you have given me the wrong word, I shall be turned back."

"I have given you the right word," interposed the major.

"If I am turned back, I shall come here first, and complete my work," added Somers, sternly.

"You shall have my pass."

"I have it already. I have not yet exhausted all my resources," said the scout, producing the two passes, which he had neglected to return in the ravine.

He opened them; but though the wounded major was surprised, he was too weak and broken in spirits to ask any questions, or even to care where his late companion had procured them.

"All I ask of you, Major Riggleston, and of you, Miss Hasbrouk, is to keep still," continued Somers.

"I will," replied Maud, eagerly.

"And I will, Captain Somers. What I have done here to save my life has ruined me. I shall never be seen in the service again."

"I think you are coming to your senses, major."

"May I ask you to keep quiet in regard to what I have done? for you know the penalty of that which I could not have done if I had not stood on the brink of the open grave."

"That will depend on your own conduct. Return to your bed; and if you are treacherous, you will suffer for it."

"I may die," groaned the major, who had sunk into a chair, for he believed his wound was much worse than it really was.

Perhaps some twinges of remorse had induced him to aid Somers in his mission more than he otherwise would; he was not a man of nerve, or a man of much nobility of purpose, and his severe wound had worked a great change in his moral and mental organization. The fear of death had deprived him of what little manliness he possessed, and under the pressure of that terror, he had sunk lower down in the scale of humanity than it would have been possible for him under any other circumstances. He had absolutely betrayed the cause for which he professed so earnest and sincere a devotion. His boasted honor was a delusion. He was an exception, even in the ranks of southern heroes.

Somers was satisfied with what was promised, and with what had already been performed. He restored his pistol to his belt, and hastened to the back room, where

Captain Barkwood was no doubt anxiously waiting to hear from him.

"Come out, captain," said he, as he threw open the door.

"Is that you, Somers?" replied the regular, as he stepped from his narrow quarters. "I had given you up for lost, and was just thinking of engaging in a little enterprise of my own. Where have you been?"

Somers, as briefly as possible, explained the events that had transpired during his absence, to which the regular listened with wonder and admiration. It was now two o'clock in the morning, and there was much still to be done before they could return to the camp. Somers, still wearing the coat and feathered hat of Major Riggleston, left the back room, followed by Barkwood, and for three hours wandered about the camps of the rebels. They were often challenged; but Somers gave his name as Major Riggleston, and produced the pass when called upon, or gave the countersign. The day was breaking in the east when they finished the examination.

## CHAPTER XIII.

### THE BATTLE OF ANTIETAM.

"WE have been detained a long time," said Somers, when they reached the ravine through which it was necessary to pass on their return; for it was not likely that the rebel pickets would permit even the ubiquitous Major Riggleston to go over to the Yankees.

"Too long, too long," replied the regular, rather nervously for him. "I am afraid we are too late to be of much service."

"The general grinds up his information rapidly. If we see him before he commences the action, we shall be all right."

Slowly and carefully they worked their way through the ravine, for they felt that they were treasure-houses of information, which must not be needlessly exposed to destruction; and a little hurrying not only imperilled their own lives, but endangered the good cause to which both of the scouts were devoted. With all the haste which the circumstances would permit, it was broad daylight when they emerged from the ravine within the Union lines.

They hurried to headquarters. Though no drums beat or bugles sounded, the note of preparation had passed silently along the lines. The orders of the general had been fully and carefully executed, and brigades and divisions were in column, ready for the advance. "Fighting Joe" and his staff were already in the saddle; and half a mile off, on a little eminence, Somers discovered the general on his white steed. Alick had groomed his horse and saddled him, though with many fears that his master would never return to use him again.

As Somers approached, the faithful fellow saw him, and led up the horse. He was overjoyed to see him once more, and made a beautiful exhibition of ivory on this interesting occasion. The young staff officer, nearly exhausted after the perils and labors of the night, filled his haversack with "hard tack," and leaped into the saddle. There was not a moment to be lost, and he dashed away towards the spot where the general was busily employed in making his preparations for the attack.

The excitement of the moment enabled him to triumph over the bodily fatigue which had weighed him down, and he urged on the noble animal he rode to his utmost speed. The horse seemed to participate in the interest and excitement of the occasion, and galloped as though he was conscious of the importance of his master's mission. As he approached the spot where the general and his staff stood, Somers reined in his steed, and nearly threw him back upon his haunches, when he raised his sword to give his commander the usual salute. It was a proud, a triumphant moment for him; and the gallant steed behaved as though it was his duty to make the utmost display as he introduced his rider to the general.

"Captain Somers!" exclaimed the general. "I gave you up this morning when I learned that you had not been heard from."

"I have the honor to report that I have fully performed the duty intrusted to me," replied Somers, employing rather more formality than usual in his address.

The scout gave his information, the most important parts of which were the fact that Stonewall Jackson's troops were concentrated on a fortified line, and that General Lee had massed his entire force behind the crests of the hill, in readiness for the great battle, which was apparently to decide the fate of the nation.

Then commenced that greatest and most momentous battle of the series of engagements in Maryland, which checked the invasion, and drove the rebels from the north to the south side of the Potomac. It was a fearful strife, a most determined battle, fought with a bravery, on both sides, bordering upon desperation. The event was to involve a mighty issue — no less than the fate of a great nation; for the moral effect of a victory by the rebels on the soil of the North would be disastrous, if not fatal, to the loyal cause, while it would open to the half starved and impoverished Confederacy the vast storehouses of wealth of the free North.

Those who fought on that day, from the skilful generals, who directed the operations, to the humblest private, who cheerfully and zealously obeyed the orders of his superiors in the midst of the terrible carnage of the battle-field, understood and appreciated the issues of that day. The sons of the republic will gratefully remember them all, and none with a more lively sense of obligation than " Fighting Joe," whose skill and judgment, no less than his heroic bravery, brought victory out of the stubborn fight intrusted to him, upon which, more than upon the operations of any other portion of the line, the fate of the day rested. He was face to face with Stonewall Jackson, the most vigorous and determined leader of the Confederacy, the pet of the rebels, and the hope of the commanding general of the invading hordes. He was pitted against this man, who was the executive of Lee's brain, without whom Lee's strategy lost its power.

The battle on the right was fought and won, but not till mighty sacrifices had been made of precious life. It was one of the most obstinate conflicts of the war; and for hours the issue swung back and forth, and it was doubtful upon which side it would rest. The first corps went forward and were driven back in places; divisions were reduced to brigades, and brigades to regiments, before the terrible fire of the rebels; and nothing but the indomitable will and the admirable skill of the general saved the day. Every weak point in the line was strengthened, every advantage was used, and every disadvantage counterbalanced, till a splendid triumph was achieved.

Stonewall Jackson was ably and prudently supported by General Lee; troops from other portions of the line were sent to this imperilled position, in a vain attempt to save the failing fortunes of the day. Fresh troops were from time to time hurled against the hard-pressed brigades of the first corps, which were forced back, but only to be again strengthened and urged on by the masterly genius of "Fighting Joe," until all that had been lost was retrieved. Later in the day, when the attack was made by the left and centre, the rebel line had been weakened by the large drafts required to meet the waste on the right, and of course the resistance was correspondingly diminished. With less stubborn and skilful fighting than that done on the right, the assaults of Burnside on the left, and of French and Richardson in the centre, could hardly have been successful.

The noble and gallant Burnside won immortal honors on that terrific day. He fought against every disadvantage, which he bravely and skilfully overcame. The result of the battle was less decisive than had been hoped and expected from the splendid fighting and the brilliant partial results achieved. The rebel army was severely handled; its resources and its *prestige* tremendously reduced; and the object of the campaign was actually accomplished; but whether the results of the several successful operations on the field were prudently agglomerated, whether the greatest practicable use was made of the victory, we must leave the historian to decide.

While Captain Somers was making his report, Captain Barkwood arrived, and was congratulated upon his safety and success. As an engineer he gave his opinion, and was able to supply information which Somers had not the scientific skill to deduce from what he had seen. The order was given to advance. The eye of the general was everywhere, even while his mind was occupied with the details furnished by the scouts. He sent members of his staff in every direction. He held the vast and complicated mechanism of his corps at his fingers' ends. He knew where every brigade and every battery of his force was at that moment, and where it was to be an hour hence. He moved them all about, as a skilful weaver tosses the many shuttles, each with a different colored thread, through the fabric before him. He was weaving history on a gigantic scale.

Somers sat upon his restless horse, eating the " hard

tack" he had brought, but ready to dash away upon any mission on which he might be sent, when an aid from the general commanding rode up and delivered an order to the commander of the corps. Somers did not particularly notice him at first, but as the staff officer turned, his teeth suddenly suspended their useful and interesting occupation, leaving his mouth half open, where it remained in the condition to express the wonder and astonishment which the presence of the officer excited.

"Major Riggleston!" exclaimed he, almost choking himself with the unmasticated block of "hard tack" in his mouth.

"Captain Somers, good morning," replied the major, with a pleasant and friendly smile.

"Is it possible?" stammered Somers.

"What possible?" demanded Riggleston.

"That you are here," replied the bewildered Somers, gazing at the major attentively, and surveying him from head to foot.

It was the same new and bright uniform which the major had worn when they met on previous occasions on the road; it was not the same which he had worn in the rebel lines, or at the Hasbrouk mansion; but the face was the same, the whiskers and mustache were the same in cut and color; and Somers, in spite of the doubt which at first assailed him, was even now ready to make oath that he was the same man he had shot in the head the preceding evening.

"Why shouldn't I be here, my dear fellow?" laughed the major. "We are going to have hot work about here to-day."

"How is your head, major?" demanded Somers, who could think of nothing at this moment but the amazing fact that he again stood in the presence of Major Riggleston.

"Cool and clear, I hope," replied the major.

"How is your wound?"

"What wound?"

"Didn't you receive a wound in the head last evening?"

"Upon my word I did not, that I am aware of."

"Will you excuse me, Major Riggleston, if I ask you to remove your hat for a moment?" said Somers, as he moved his horse up to the side of the major's.

"Certainly; with pleasure," replied the staff officer, as he took off his hat.

There was no bandage, nor any appearance of a wound. Somers was more bewildered than ever, and was disposed to do what heroes in the romances do when anything looks astonishingly mysterious — ascribe the delusion to a dream. But he was tired enough from the exertions of the night to convince him that all which had occurred within the rebel lines was a reality.

"Will you allow me to examine your head?" asked he, utterly unable to see through the dark problem.

"I will do even that with pleasure, Captain Somers; though I think you are a little beside yourself," laughed the major.

Somers reached forward, and put his hand on the part of the major's head where the pistol ball had struck him; but there was not the slightest abrasion of the skin; in a word, the head was in good order and condition, and it was absolutely certain that no bullet had passed through his skull.

"I am satisfied, Major Riggleston," replied Somers, though he was still in a bewildered state of mind. "I owe you an apology for the rude treatment to which I subjected you on a former occasion. You are not the man I took you to be; and I hope you will pardon my rough speech and unfriendly manners."

"Cheerfully, Captain Somers. Here is my hand," replied the major, evidently as much pleased to forgive as the scout was to be forgiven.

"I am satisfied now."

"But I am not," responded the major.

"Last night, about eleven o'clock, I shot you through the head," said Somers, facetiously.

"Me!"

"Yes, you!"

"Well, perhaps you did; but I did not feel it."

"I was willing, a moment ago, to give my affidavit that you were the person. I was mistaken this time, as

I was yesterday when I accused you of being a traitor. By the way, Major Riggleston," added Somers, as he took from his pocket the two passes he had received from the mysterious personage in the ravine, and selecting the Union one, handed it to his companion, " is this document yours?"

" It is," replied the major, glancing at the pass. " Where did you get this?"

" Is this yours?" continued Somers, handing him the other pass.

" No; this is a rebel pass," answered the major. " I never saw it before, and have no occasion for a paper of this description. Where did you get the other?"

" You gave it to me last night," laughed Somers.

" I'm sure I did not."

" Captain Somers," called the general; and the interview was abruptly terminated.

## CHAPTER XIV.

#### THE BATTLE ON THE RIGHT.

THE Pennsylvania Reserves, commanded by General Meade, occupied the centre of the line of the first corps. They were a noble body of troops, and had done some of the most splendid fighting of the war on the Peninsula, and in the bloody but indecisive battles of Pope's campaign. Captain Somers, as if in compliment to him for his zeal and his energy, was sent to bear the order for this division to advance.

The Reserves moved forward with a hearty, cheerful zeal; and presently the thunder of their artillery, and the rattling volleys of musketry, proclaimed the commencement of the conflict. A portion of Stonewall Jackson's command was before them — men who always fought with the energy of desperation. They were a worthy foe, and worthily were they met; but the rebels had the advantage. Their renowned leader had chosen their position, and the brave Pennsylvanians suffered terribly.

"Fighting Joe," on his white charger, rode up to the

position in the front of the battle. He was calm and unmoved in the shower of bullets, and the troops were gladdened and encouraged by his presence. They were strong without him; they were stronger with him. He gave off his orders with the utmost coolness, and spoke words of fire, which burned in the souls of the men. He was there, — the idol of the army, — and there was not a man who would not have been ashamed to skulk with this noble example before him. The mighty will of the general was communicated to the nerves and the muscles of his soldiers, and he multiplied himself thousands of times in the persons of his devoted followers.

Still they moved on, Meade's division, supported by that of Ricketts, nearer to the woods where the rebels were concentrated; and still they poured in the deadly volleys, until the resistance before them was sensibly diminished.

"Forward!" was the word that rang along the line; and the Reserves, supported by two of Ricketts's brigades, rushed on with cheers, and entered the oak grove. The rebels were falling back before them, and they rushed through the woods, across the open field on the other side, and still onward to the woods beyond the field. But here they were thrown upon bodies of fresh troops, hurried up to meet them. From the dark shadows of the wood came showers of bullets from a sheet of flaming fire. The grove was packed with rebels; the Reserves seemed to melt away like frost before the sunlight, in that galling fire. They closed up their shattered lines, and fell doggedly back, pouring in volley after volley upon the dense masses.

The fortunes of the day seemed suddenly to have been reversed; what had been victory a moment before, now became defeat. Stonewall Jackson's entire line was advancing with those fiendish yells which distinguish the rebel onslaught. It was a critical moment in the fortunes of the day; but the genius of the man who held the reins in his hands was equal to the occasion. He was not a mile in the rear; he was in the front, where he could see the indications of threatening disaster; where he could promptly meet and counteract the elements of defeat which had begun to manifest themselves.

"Captain Somers," said he, in his calm but earnest tones.

Somers spurred forward his horse, and saluting the general, stood in readiness for his commands.

"Tell General Ricketts to send me his best brigade instantly."

It rained shot and shell on the hill-side as Somers dashed away to execute the order. Presently the "best brigade," consisting of the twelfth and thirteenth Massachusetts, the ninth New York, and the eleventh Pennsylvania, under the command of General Hartsuff, double-quicked down the hill, amid the falling shot and bursting shell, which crashed fearfully through the trees, and tore up the earth in their mad flight. They were veteran troops, commanded by a veteran soldier of skill and bravery. They passed the general on their march, and his eye lighted up with satisfaction as he saw the spirit which they manifested.

"I think they will hold the ground," said he, as General Hartsuff, passing the shattered lines of the Reserves, drew up his brigade on the summit of a hill between them and the exultant foe.

They fired in volleys at first, and then at will; but they did their work most heroically. None flinched; none fled. The rebels pushed forward their flushed troops; but these gallant fellows stormed them with bullets, and, assisted by the brigades of Gibbons and Patrick, repelled the assault. Jackson's line suffered severely, and a large number of field officers were killed in vain attempts to rally them. The rebels fell back again to the woods from which they had come, and again this part of the line was safe. There had been a terrible loss in the gallant brigade which held the brow of the hill, and General Hartsuff was severely wounded early in the action.

The general of the corps had saved his line in this place — had brought a success out of a reverse; but his brain was still active. Batteries rushed like a train of meteors over the field, obedient to his ready thought.

Messages of varied import came to him from division commanders. Ricketts was hard pressed — could barely hold his position; and a portion of Mansfield's corps was sent to his aid. The venerable soldier went with two of his brigades; but he was mortally wounded, and was borne to the rear.

"Go to that regiment on the right, Captain Somers, and tell the colonel not to let his men break on any account," said the general.

Somers dashed away, and stood before broken fragments of a regiment, with hardly a commissioned officer left in the line. They were noble and brave fellows, and they were yielding only when there seemed to be no one left to lead them. They were giving way, and making a gap in the line, through which the desperate rebels could burst, and overwhelm the column.

The staff officer saw at a glance the state of the case. He blamed not the men; it was the fault of the cowardly officer upon whom the command had devolved. He was weak and inefficient; at least he was not man enough for such a trying emergency.

"The general desires to hold this line, at all hazards," said Somers, saluting the officer. "Where is the general of this brigade?"

"He has got his hands full yonder," replied the captain in command of the regiment.

"You must hold this position without fail."

"Can't hold it."

"Yes, you can!" exclaimed Somers, fiercely.

"I can't hold it any longer."

"Forward, my brave boys. The day is ours if we stand up to it a little while longer!" shouted he to the hard-pressed troops, whose thin ranks were rapidly becoming thinner under the fierce fire to which they were subjected. "Follow me!" he added, in clarion tones, as he swung his sword in the air.

A faint cheer burst from the ranks of the regiment, showing that they had not wholly lost their spirit. They clutched their muskets tighter, and looked sternly towards the rebel line.

"Don't spoil your record for this day, my gallant fellows," continued Somers. "You have done gloriously; stick to it to the end."

"Who are you?" said a gruff fellow in the ranks.

"Captain Somers, of the general's staff. He expects you to hold this line. He sent me down to you. Shall I tell him you are a pack of cowards? Or shall I tell him you have done your duty, and been cut to pieces in the place where he put you?"

"You bet!" added the gruff fellow. "Come, boys!"

"Follow me!" shouted Somers, as he urged his foaming steed through the ranks, and waved his sword over his head.

"He's the chap! Go in, boys," cried one of the men,

as the ranks closed up, and they followed the intrepid staff officer back to the position from which they had retreated.

The rebels had seen the break, and were swift to take advantage of it. They rushed forward, whooping like savages; but the fragmentary regiment now stood like a wall of iron, and poured a volley into the advancing horde, before which they quailed, and then retreated.

"Bravo! my noble fellows. 'Fighting Joe' is looking at you, and he shall know all about it."

"Hurrah!" shouted the brave men, who had gathered new life and hope from the inspiring words of the young staff officer.

"You will stand firm — won't you?" demanded Somers.

"Hurrah!" yelled the reorganized, revivified little force, so heartily that Somers fell back from the front to return to his position at the side of the general.

"Captain Somers!" said a familiar voice, almost in a yell. "Somers, by all that is grand and beautiful!"

Somers turned, and saw a man approaching him from the ranks of an adjoining regiment. He was dressed in the uniform of an officer, but he had a musket in his hand. He was begrimed with smoke, and his cheek was blackened by close contact with the piece in his hand.

"Major de Banyan!" replied Somers, as his old friend

rushed up to his side, and seized his hand. "What are you doing here?"

"I happened up here on business, and I went in as a volunteer on my own hook," replied De Banyan, still shaking the hand of the staff officer, though the bullets were whistling, and the shot and shell were roaring around him.

"That's like you. Have you no position?"

"I am a private, just now."

"By order of the general commanding the first corps, I place you in command of this broken regiment," said Somers, not doubting that he could soon procure a confirmation of his deed.

"Good! that reminds me —"

"No, it don't; no what-you-call-ems," laughed Somers.

"You are right, Somers. I have hardly told a story since we parted."

At this moment the brigadier general rode up, and Somers referred the matter of the command to him. When he learned what had happened, he installed Major de Banyan in the temporary charge of the regiment. Somers said a few words to the boys, to reconcile them to their new commander. He told them who and what De Banyan was; the major stepped in front of them, and went to work with his usual skill and bravery. Somers left his friend, with a promise to see him again as soon as possible, and rode back to the general.

There was a certain piece of woods on the right which the general regarded as the key to the position, and which he had determined to take and to hold. He was in the act of riding forward for the purpose of examining this point in person, as he did on all important occasions. Somers reported to him just as he was leaving the front of the most advanced line of troops. He continued his bold reconnoissance till he reached the top of the hill, where he dismounted, and went forward on foot. He coolly and carefully surveyed the ground, returned to his horse, and remounted.

The storm of musket balls from the point of woods was kept up all this time with the most determined vigor. The erect, manly form of "Fighting Joe" had been conspicuous on the field all the morning, and the rebels had fired at him individually hundreds of times; but he seemed to have a charmed life. He had been spared to complete the work he had begun, and which he had so ably and successfully carried forward.

As he mounted his horse he sent Somers off on a mission to the batteries of artillery planted on the ridge behind him. It was in the midst of one of the hottest fires of the day. Three men dropped near the general. He turned and started for another part of the field; but he had hardly advanced a pace before he was struck in the foot by a rifle ball.

"You are wounded, general," said Somers, returning to the spot.

"Carry the order I gave you, Captain Somers," replied he, with an expression of pain on his noble features.

Somers galloped off to execute his mission.

The general still sat his horse, and gave directions for the capture and holding of the point he had examined at the peril of his precious life. The surgeon advised him to leave the field, but he refused to do so. He swayed backward and forward, reeling from faintness in his saddle. Still he looked about him, to carry out the purpose which filled his mind.

"There's a regiment on the right of us. Order it forward! Crawford and Gordon are coming up. Tell them to take those woods, and hold them; and it is *our* fight!" said he, feebly, but with emphasis.

He fainted, but partially recovered, and rode slowly and reluctantly to the rear, after he had sent word to General Sumner that he was wounded.

## CHAPTER XV.

### AFTER THE BATTLE.

GENERAL SUMNER was close at hand with his corps. He saw the wounded commander, spoke to him, and passed on to complete the work which had been so far accomplished, apparently, that it only remained to hold what had already been gained.

"Fighting Joe" had virtually contended with the whole rebel army, for the attack on the left and in the centre was delayed for hours after the victory on the right had been won. He had done his part in the day's work nobly and successfully; and there his responsibility for the results of the battle terminated.

Somers went to the rear with his wounded general, but, when assured that the injury, though very severe, was not dangerous, and that he could be of no service to him, returned to the field, resolved to act as a volunteer. There was heavy fighting in the woods, where Crawford and Gordon were executing the last order of the commander of the first corps. The rebels, by the delay in the Union attack on the left and centre, were enabled to send forward fresh troops; and the combat deepened until the woods blazed with fire.

The young staff officer rushed in, and hastily reported to General Crawford as a volunteer. He was cordially thanked, his services accepted, and he was directed to use his own judgment. There were plenty of exhausted regiments vainly struggling to roll back the tide of defeat which was setting fiercely against them. Hundreds of gallant officers lay dead and wounded upon the ground, and there was abundance of work for any brave leader who had the nerve to do it.

Somers attempted to rally the broken ranks, and close up the wide gaps which had been made by the fearful carnage; but Crawford was forced back, and what had been gained on the front was lost. At this crisis General Franklin came up with fresh troops, and the ground which had been lost was regained, not to be again abandoned.

The excitement was over, and Somers began to think that he had a body as well as a spirit. He was thoroughly exhausted when he left the field of his last labor, and rode over to the point where he had left Major de Banyan.

"What's the matter, my dear boy?" demanded the major, as he rode up to the begrimed soldier. "Are you wounded?"

"No," replied Somers, languidly; but he hardly knew what did ail him.

"You are as pale as death. Are you sure you are not wounded?" asked the major, tenderly and anxiously.

"I don't think I am."

"Dismount, and let me overhaul you. I'm sure you are in a bad condition," continued the veteran, as he took the hand of the staff officer.

"I don't feel very well," added Somers.

Things began to look very shaky before him; he felt a deadly nausea; and before he could get off his horse, he sank fainting into the arms of his friend. The major took him from his saddle and laid him on the ground. He was alarmed, and tore open his coat to examine the vital parts of his body; but there was no wound, or even a spot of blood to indicate one. He procured a canteen of water, sprinkled his face, and rubbed his temples with his hands.

Captain Somers had only fainted from exhaustion consequent upon the severe trials of the preceding night, and the excitement and fatigue he had undergone during the battle. The skilful attentions of De Banyan soon restored him to consciousness; but he was as weak and feeble as an infant. He had eaten only one of the biscuits he had taken in the morning, and had performed his trying duties on an empty stomach. His health, already shattered, was not equal to the fatigues he had been called upon to endure.

"There is nothing further for you or me to do here.

We have won the field, and if the rest of the line does its work we shall have the day," said De Banyan. "Now we will go and have you taken care of."

"I am willing, for I can't stand this any longer," replied Somers, feebly.

The major helped him on his horse again, and walked by his side, as they slowly made their way to the rear. Every house in the vicinity of the battle-field was filled with wounded soldiers, and there was no spot where De Banyan could find a resting-place for his patient; but he obtained some refreshment for him, which in a measure restored his strength.

"I'm afraid you are going to be sick, Somers," said the major, anxiously, as he gazed upon the pale face of his friend.

"I feel so myself."

"I am bound to see you in a comfortable place. Do you know of one?"

"The farther we go from this vicinity, the more likely we shall be to find one. I must report myself at headquarters first."

"Right; and you will find your servant there."

They went to the place where the headquarters had been located, but the wounded general had been conveyed to Centreville. Somers, however, reported himself to the chief of staff, and found Alick.

"Major de Banyan, as sure as you was born!" exclaimed the servant.

"I'm glad to see you, Alick," returned the major. "Your master is sick, and we must look out for him."

"Yes, sar," replied the faithful fellow, who proceeded at once to saddle the extra horse.

As yet nothing had been or could be learned of the result of the battle; and the little party moved off in search of accommodations for the sick officer. De Banyan declared that he must get away from the terrible scenes of death and mutilation in the neighborhood of the battle-field. He was physician enough to understand that the nerves of his patient were much shattered, and that he needed absolute quiet.

"I know a house which I think must be deserted," said Somers; "but it is eight or ten miles off."

"So much the better, if you can manage to get there," replied De Banyan, who was mounted on Somers's spare horse, while Alick walked in the rear.

"I should not be very welcome there."

"No matter for that. I will take possession of the place in the name of the United States of America. After the battle of Magenta — there was a quiet time, I suppose," laughed the major. "Where is the place you speak of?"

"It is the Hasbrouk mansion." And as they rode slowly along, Somers told his companion of the exciting events which had occurred there, and of those which had followed it since his arrival in Maryland.

In return De Banyan related the incidents which had happened in the —th Massachusetts, of which Somers was still an officer; of its march from the Peninsula, and its terrible baptism of blood at Groveton, where Captain Benson had fallen mortally wounded; and other red fields in which the regiments had been reduced to a mere skeleton. There were a thousand things for each to tell, and Somers almost forgot his weakness in the interest he felt in the history of his company and his regiment.

"But, Somers, how is that pretty young lady who used to knit stockings?" asked the major.

"She is well; I saw her the day I left Boston. I have that same pair of socks on my feet now. I put them on yesterday, when we went forward."

"Well, but how do you get on?"

"Get on?"

"Bah! You know what I mean."

"I'm sure I don't," replied Somers, faintly, though a soft blush colored his pale cheek.

"You are courting, of course."

"That's nonsense."

"I know it's nonsense; but young fellows like you are given to such folly."

"I'm not."

"Pooh!"

"She's my friend, and I am hers."

"Of course you are."

"Her father is a rich merchant, and I am nothing but a poor boy. I have no idea of any such thing as you speak of."

"Haven't you, indeed? Let me tell you, Somers, if she was the daughter of the President of the United States, she isn't any too good for you; and if she's offish on that score, I should like the privilege of telling her so," added the major, with no little spirit.

"That's nonsense, major."

"If Miss — What's her name, Somers?"

"Lilian Ashford."

"That's an amazing pretty name, Somers. If she's too good to marry a brigadier general, and such a brigadier general as — "

"I'm not a brigadier."

"But you will be before the war is over."

"I shall not; you are absurd, major."

"Perhaps I am."

"I don't feel now as though I should be anything much longer."

"Don't give it up, my boy; you will be as good as new in a week or two."

"I promised to write to Lilian."

"Good! Do it, then."

"I have no hopes in that quarter. We are only friends. I like her very well, but we don't talk of anything but those socks."

"I say, Somers, when you are a brigadier, and have made your fortune, you will want a coat of arms. Let me suggest one."

"A coat of arms!" laughed Somers.

"Certainly; you will want one. All great men have one."

"And you would put a pair of socks on it?"

"Certainly; that's the idea. But where are we going, Somers?"

"To the Hasbrouk mansion; and we are nearly there," replied the sick man.

Somers had chosen this place on account of its retired situation, and because he could think of no other suitable house to be sick in. In spite of his cheerful nature, he had some dismal forebodings in regard to the future. Nothing but the inspiration of his lively companion's presence kept him from sinking under the pain and weakness which assailed him. On the road, by the prudent counsels of his friend, he had stopped several times to rest and refresh himself. He had never felt so weak and shattered before, and he feared it would be many a long day before he was able again to take his place on the staff of the general, or in the line of his regiment.

In the middle of the afternoon, while the guns were still thundering at Antietam, the little party reached the Hasbrouk mansion. Major de Banyan took upon himself the whole charge of gaining admission; and, with his usual bold front, he entered without knocking. The family, which had left the house while hostilities were in progress around it, had now returned. Alick took the horses, and Somers followed the major into the mansion. To the surprise of both they were immediately confronted by Maud, who had moved her patients to her own home, when the battle commenced, early in the morning.

De Banyan politely stated his business, at the same time acting as though his stay was a settled thing, whether the family were willing or not.

"We cannot accommodate you, sir," replied Maud, as haughtily as though she had been the queen of "my Maryland."

"Sorry for it, miss; but I shall be obliged to take possession."

"We have three wounded officers here now," added she.

"They are rebels."

"They are Confederate officers, sir, or they would not be here."

"There will be one here who is not a Confederate officer. My friend, Captain Somers, must be accommodated; and I shall be obliged to turn out the rebel officers, unless you can find room for him without my doing so."

"I will not submit to this insolence!" exclaimed she, rushing out of the room.

"Good! Now wait till I find a room for you, Somers."

"I would not have come here if I had not supposed the house was deserted. I feel faint again, major."

"Don't faint just yet."

De Banyan made himself entirely at home; brought water, cologne, a smelling-bottle, and finally set up his friend for another brief period. He then went up stairs, selected a front room, which, from its contents, was evidently the apartment of Maud herself. He set Alick at work in the chamber making a fire, and otherwise preparing it for the reception of the sick officer.

The major then conducted his patient to the comfortable quarters he had secured, and put him to bed. All the house could furnish he obtained, with or without leave, and did all he could to improve the condition of his sick friend. At night Somers was in a raging fever, and the major was greatly alarmed at his condition.

## CHAPTER XVI.

#### THE MYSTERY EXPLAINED.,

CAPTAIN SOMERS knew very little of what took place at the Hasbrouk mansion within the next three weeks, being delirious during the greater portion of this time. Major de Banyan conquered a peace with the family within twenty-four hours, and obtained all that he required in the service of the sick man without fighting for it. An old but skilful physician was procured, who pronounced the disease a severe case of typhoid fever, which presented many alarming symptoms.

The major was a tender and a skilful nurse; but he felt that another presence than his own was necessary in the sick room. The sufferer needed the soothing care of woman, and De Banyan sent a letter to Pinchbrook, containing a full statement of the alarming condition of the captain; and at the end of a week his mother came, attended by his father.

The Hasbrouk family, though cold and unsympathizing towards their unwelcome guests, afforded Mrs. Somers every convenience for the discharge of her motherly duty. De Banyan, when compelled by the expiration of his furlough to return to his regiment, distinctly informed Maud and her father, if any disrespect was shown to Mrs. Somers or her husband, or any hinderance thrown in their way, he would cause them all to be turned out of the house, and do his best to have the property immediately confiscated. The threat had the desired effect, and though Mrs. Somers could not help feeling that she was an intruder on the premises, her discomfort was not increased by any misconduct on the part of the host or his family.

For days Somers's life seemed to hang only by a thread. His devoted mother trembled over him during the long and weary nights. She and her husband, assisted by the faithful Alick, took the whole care of the sufferer, rarely seeing any member of the family. A separate table was set for them, and their presence was avoided as though they carried the pestilence in their garments. They were the "mud-sills" of the North, and there could be no communication between them.

At the end of three weeks, the danger had passed away, and the patient began to improve. In a short time, under the skilful care of the old doctor, he was able to go down stairs; and his father at once made arrangements for removing him to his home in Pinchbrook, anxious to escape as soon as possible from the cold hospitality of the Hasbrouks. On the day before the intended departure, a servant announced that Major Riggleston wished to see him, and would meet him in the parlor. Attended by his mother, he went down stairs.

"I am glad to see you, Captain Somers, but sorry to find you so ill," said the major, when Mrs. Somers had been duly introduced.

"Thank you, major; I have had rather a rough time of it."

"You were fortunate in having the attentions of your good mother."

"I should have died without her," added the captain, glancing affectionately at his mother.

"Well, we don't know about those things, Thomas," said Mrs. Somers, meekly.

"I learned that you were here three weeks ago, and I intended to call upon you before this time," continued the major. "You know there was a little affair between us that needed clearing up."

"It would done no good to come much afore now; the poor boy wan't fit to be seen. He's had an awful hard time on't, and nothing but almighty Power has kept him from the grave," interposed Mrs. Somers, wiping away the tear that started in her eye when she thought of the days in which her son was trembling between life and death. "If I can only once get him home, he shan't leave me again. He went off afore when he was no more fit to go than a baby."

"The captain is a very useful person in the army."

"Well, I suppose he is; but there's no sense nor reason in his going off when he ain't fit to go. We shall get away from here to-morrow."

"My mother don't like this place very well," said Somers, with a smile. "The people here are not remarkably fond of me."

"Why not?"

"I forgot that you did not know anything about it. I will tell you now, Major Riggleston, and I'm sure you will not blame me for the rude words I spoke to you, when you understand the matter."

"You did the fair thing when you discovered your mistake; but you spoke to your general about the affair, and he does not regard me with favor. I came over here partly for the purpose of affording you an opportunity to clear me from the imputation that rests upon my honor. An explanation from you will set the matter right."

"I can't explain it myself," added Somers. "I only know that you are not the man who entrapped me, and whom I shot in the head."

Somers then related the history of the affair in the house where they were then assembled, and that which occurred in the rebel lines. Major Riggleston listened to the narrative with deep interest, as did Mrs. Somers, whose husband had gone with Alick to examine the battle-field of Antietam and South Mountain.

"Sakes alive! who ever heard of such things!" exclaimed Mrs. Somers, when her son had finished his exciting story. "It's a wonder that you wan't killed, Thomas."

"I understand it all now, Captain Somers," said the major, rather disconcerted. "Though I am not at all to blame in the premises, the affair more nearly concerns me than you may suppose."

"I exonerate you entirely, Major Riggleston," continued Somers.

"There, Thomas, you musn't talk any more now," interposed the matron.

"I won't say anything more, but I must settle this affair, mother."

At this moment the door opened, and Maud Hasbrouk was on the point of entering; but when she saw that the parlor was already occupied, she turned to retire.

"These people in here!" said she, contemptuously, but loud enough to be heard by all in the room.

"No matter, Maud; go in if Ernest is there," said another person, behind her.

"He is there; he is a friend of Captain Somers," sneered she, as she walked into the apartment as though she had been a superior being.

"How is your health, Captain Somers?" asked the person who followed Maud.

He was an officer, and his head was tied up with a bandage.

"Major Riggleston!" exclaimed Somers, starting from his chair.

"Goodness!" ejaculated Mrs. Somers, fearful that the excitement her son exhibited would throw him into another fever. "What ails the boy?"

"You are certainly the person at whom I fired," added Somers, as he gazed at the form and features of the new comer.

"No doubt of that, Captain Somers," replied the major. "And a very nice time I've had of it too."

"I hope some one will serve you in the same way," said Maud, spitefully.

"For massy sake!" exclaimed Mrs. Somers, fearful in the gathering events that some one would serve her darling boy in the same way. "What has Thomas done?"

"He is a —"

"Not another word, Maud," said the wounded major, sternly. "He did his duty, and I am not the one to blame him for it."

"I hope you will do yours, major, if the circumstances ever place you in the same situation."

"I should; and Captain Somers would not blame me for it."

"Certainly not," replied Somers.

"He saved your life and mine, Maud; and we will not quarrel now."

The proud beauty was silent and sullen, while Somers gazed in wonder from one Major Riggleston to the other Major Riggleston.

"You understand it now, Captain Somers?" said the loyal major.

"I do; it is all very plain now. You must acknowledge that I made a very natural mistake."

"It is not the first time I have been taken for my brother. He is two years older than I am; but we look very much alike."

When they were together, several points of difference could be observed; and the resemblance was not now so great as it had been before the battle of Antietam, for the rebel major had grown thinner and paler under the suffering induced by his wound. At the time Somers had met them, the similarity in form and features, in voice and manner, was so great, that a person of ordinary perception, meeting them at different times, could not have told one from the other. The rebel major had changed so much during his illness that the difference was now more perceptible.

"It never occurred to me that you had seen my brother," said Major Fred, who was the loyal brother. "If it had, I should have understood the whole matter."

"I understood it perfectly," added Major Ernest, who was the rebel brother. "I confess, too, that I took advantage of the circumstance."

"But where did you get my safe-conduct?" asked Fred.

"I picked it up the night we were at home," replied Ernest, rather sheepishly.

"That was hardly fair."

"All fair in war, Fred."

"Well, then, it is one of the disadvantages of having a brother on the wrong side, Ernest."

"That name, Ernest, reminds me that I heard it at your father's house, in Frederick," added Somers.

"Captain Somers," said the loyal major, very seriously, "you may think I am not as patriotic as I ought to be. You know that my brother was at my father's house, and that I saw him there. You may think I ought to have handed him over as a prisoner of war."

"Thomas don't think any such thing," said Mrs. Somers.

"I have nothing to say about that; it is a family affair," added Captain Somers. "I need only say that I regard you, Major Fred Riggleston, as a loyal man; and I shall write the general a letter containing a full explanation of my blunder."

"Thank you, captain," replied Fred. "That will set me right."

"By the way, Captain Somers," said the rebel major, "there is a matter between us also."

"What I agreed in honor and confidence to do, I have done, and shall continue to do," replied Somers, alluding to the matter of the rebel countersign, imparted to him by the wounded major.

"There, Thomas, you musn't say another word," interposed Mrs. Somers, once more.

Maud left the room, disgusted with the proceedings, and dissatisfied with the conduct of her lover, who persistently refused to revile the Yankees present. When she had gone, Major Ernest walked up to Somers, and in a low tone, remarked that he should never again serve in the rebel army. The captain commended his resolution, and hoped he would be able to do more and better than this, and be found in the ranks of his country's defenders in the hour of peril. He shook his head, and made no reply.

Somers was conducted to his chamber by his mother, who insisted that he should lie down; for she greatly feared the effects of the excitement to which he had been subjected. Late in the evening, Captain Somers, senior, returned from the battle-fields, and his wife regaled him for an hour with the adventures of their son, concerning which, Captain Somers, junior, had up to this day preserved a discreet silence.

On the following day, Somers, with his parents,

started for home. The feeble condition of the invalid compelled them to travel very slowly, and remain two or three days at each of the principal cities through which they passed on the journey. Consequently it was nearly a fortnight before they reached Pinchbrook, where the hero was duly welcomed; and where, in a few days after his arrival, he had the happiness to receive a visit from Lilian Ashford.

She was as gentle and beautiful as ever, and smiled so sweetly upon him, and pitied him so tenderly, that he almost found it in his heart to rejoice at the suffering which had procured him such a blissful meeting. Lilian told him how disappointed her grandmother was at not seeing him, as he had promised, and that she still lived in the hope of meeting him. Of course Somers proposed to keep the broken engagement as soon as he was able to visit the city.

Lilian was accompanied by her father, who manifested a hearty interest in the young aid-de-camp, and joined warmly with his daughter in the invitation to visit his house. This was hopeful, and afforded Somers many pleasant reflections, the nature of which we need hardly explain to our cunning readers. The visitors departed, and the invalid's suffering body contained a hopeful spirit.

## CHAPTER XVII.

#### DOWN IN TENNESSEE.

*I*T was four months before Captain Somers was able to visit Boston, so severely had his constitution been shattered by the fatigues of the service, and by the strain of exciting events upon his nervous system. Lilian Ashford and her father visited Pinchbrook several times during this period, and an excellent understanding was established between the captain and the young lady. The visit was returned in the spring, when Somers was able to endure the fatigue; and as his health gradually improved, he repeated his calls till they occurred as often as once a week.

Grandmother Ashford had abundant opportunity now to tell all about the "last war," and Somers listened with the attention which so interesting a narrative deserved. Perhaps it was fortunate for the venerable lady that her eyesight was impaired, or she might have been wounded to observe that her patient auditor looked more at Lilian than at herself. On one of these occasions the old lady was so imprudent as to leave the young couple in the parlor, and something passed between them which seemed to make Somers very much pleased with himself and with Lilian, and to make Lilian equally well pleased with herself and with Somers. What this was, the experienced reader may possibly be able to divine; but as our story relates mainly to the military history of our hero, it cannot properly be introduced.

Captain Somers was certainly improving in health, but so slowly that there was no present prospect of his being able to join his regiment, or report on the staff of his beloved general, now commanding the grand army of the Potomac. His physician positively refused to permit him even to visit the scene of active operations; and after communicating with "Fighting Joe" by letter, he decided to resign his position in the —th Massachusetts, for his continued absence not only deprived the regiment of his services, but prevented some deserving officer, who performed his duties, from receiving the pay and promotion to which he was justly entitled. But he did not take this decisive step till he was assured by the general that he could have an appointment on the staff as soon as he was able to discharge the duties of the position.

While Somers was absent from the army, the great battle of Fredericksburg had been fought; and the brave, noble, and Christian Burnside, perplexed by the treachery of seeming friends, by the over-zealous movements of real ones, and by the machinations of envious and jealous officers, who should have been foremost to support him, was badly defeated. The rank and file behaved nobly, fought well, and the day ought to have been won; but the parts of the grand army were disjointed; they did not act in concert; and portions of the force were left to be mercilessly slaughtered. The devoted and unselfish Burnside shouldered the responsibility, and stepped down from the exalted military pinnacle to which he had been raised without ambition, and against his own desires.

He was succeeded by Major General Hooker, the "bravest of the brave," and one of the ablest soldiers which the war had developed. He had fought and lost the great battle of Chancellorsville; but he, too, was a victim of jealousy and indecision on the part of men whose purposes were their own, instead of their suffering country's.

The culminating battle of the war was fought at Gettysburg by his successor. It was a decisive victory; for the defiant foe was penetrating the heart of the North, and there could be no trifling with the terrible fact that stared the nation full in the face. The generals and the army fought nobly, and the exulting rebels were hurled back, shattered and discomfited, to the soil of Virginia.

The battle of Gettysburg was immediately followed by the surrender of Vicksburg and Port Hudson; and operations in the West and South-west attracted the attention of the country during the remainder of the year, while the army of the Potomac was comparatively quiet in Virginia. The battle of Chickamauga Creek was fought, and the Union army defeated, and only saved from disaster by the skill and firmness of General Thomas.

The Confederate authorities, taking advantage of the lull in the storm of battle in the East, sent General Longstreet and his corps to the West, which being understood in Washington, the eleventh and twelfth corps of the army of the Potomac were despatched, under command of General Hooker, to counteract this addition to the force of the rebels.

Captain Somers had impatiently watched the progress of events in the East and in the West, and mourned over the necessity which compelled him to remain inactive. He had attended to his health, and felt that he was completely restored, even before his stubborn physician would acknowledge the fact. But in the month of September, when he had been nearly a year off duty, the doctor gave him a " clean bill of health." He had employed much of his time, since his strength would permit, in athletic exercises — in rowing, in gymnastics, and in hard labor in the garden. He was heavier and stronger than he had ever been before, and he was ashamed to remain any longer in idleness when the country needed his arm. He wrote to the general again, just as the stalwart hero was on the point of starting for the West.

Three days after, Somers received a reply, informing him that in a short time he would receive a commission as a captain in the regular army, and an appointment on his staff as senior aid-de-camp. To this agreeable intelligence was added the hardly less agreeable fact that Major de Banyan and Captain Barkwood would also be members of his military family.

"Glory, hallelujah!" shouted Somers, as he rushed into the humble cottage at Pinchbrook.

"What on airth is the matter now, Thomas?" asked his mother, dropping the wet dish-cloth on the floor in her astonishment.

"Read that, mother!" shouted the captain.

"I hain't got my glasses, Thomas. What is it?"

"A captain in the regular army! A soldier for life. What will Lilian say to that?"

"Dear me! Well, that is news," added Mrs. Somers, who, however, was not very clear in regard to the distinction between a regular and a volunteer officer. "I suppose the gal will think you are a pretty smart boy. I hope it won't make you proud and vain, Thomas."

"I'm proud, mother; but I guess it won't make me vain. I tell you what, it's no small thing to be a captain in the regular army. I think Lilian won't like me any less for this."

"Cat's foot! She won't like you any more. If she does, she ain't the gal I take her to be. Do you suppose she will want you off all the time, when you —"

"Come, mother, you are getting ahead of my time," said the young captain, with a blush. "Well, I wish the papers would come, for I am in a hurry to be at work again."

"They'll come soon enough," added the mother, sadly, as she thought of another long separation, and the dismal hours that would be spent in waiting for intelligence of him after a battle had been fought.

The next day came a long letter from De Banyan, in which he congratulated himself and his friend on the prospect before them, and proposed to meet him at Louisville on the journey to the new field of operations. The commission and the appointment soon followed, and Somers again donned his staff uniform. The hardest thing before him was to leave home, which had become doubly endeared to him by his long stay. He had seen his twin brother, now in the navy, during a brief visit the latter made to Pinchbrook, when sent to Boston as prize-master of a brig he had captured. This was the only time they had met since the departure of Thomas, at the commencement of the war.

Mrs. Somers was a woman of tender feelings, and she

wept bitterly as she again bade her son adieu, and gave him into the keeping of the almighty Father, who had protected and preserved him through so many perils. In Boston, as may well be supposed, he hastened to the house of Mr. Ashford, and saw Lilian, who had already been informed of his intended departure. She now had a deeper interest in him than ever before; and she was sad, but hopeful. Another earnest prayer to God for his safety was to be added daily and nightly to those which went up from the humble home in Pinchbrook.

"Do you see this bundle, Lilian?" said Somers, as he opened the parcel in his hand.

"What is it?"

"Don't you see?"

"Socks!"

"They are the banner under, or, rather, over, which I fight," said he, handing her the articles.

"They are hardly worn at all," replied she, with a sad smile.

"But they have been on my feet in every battle in which I have been engaged. I never wear them except in a fight, for I don't want to wear them out."

"I will knit you some more."

"But they would not be these, if you did," laughed Somers, trying to be as cheerful as possible. "These socks have helped me to do my duty; and they introduced me to you, which is the best part of it. When the war is over, I am going to put them in a glass case, and keep them in my room, to remind me of the scenes of the past."

"You are a funny fellow, Thomas," said she.

"Perhaps I am; but I mean all I say."

A great deal more was said, which we are afraid would look very silly to some wise and prudent people, if we should transfer it to our page; but the words spoken by both were very earnest and sincere, though perhaps they were rather sentimental, as might have been naturally expected under such circumstances. He spoke the good by, and left the house. He did not see the tears shed by Lilian after he had gone. More than her words, even, they told of her sincerity. Mr. Ashford was not at home when he called, and Somers paid his respects to him at his counting-room. The wealthy merchant was deeply interested in him, and readily accepted the fact which the intimacy between his daughter and the young soldier indicated.

Followed by the prayers and the hopes of devoted friends, he proceeded on his journey to the West. Alick, who had been at work in Pinchbrook during the year, accompanied him as his servant. In due time he reached Louisville, where, in conformity with the arrangement, he met Major de Banyan, and together they repaired to Nashville. They had brought with them their saddles, and other military equipments, but it was necessary to procure horses at this place.

The headquarters of the eleventh and twelfth corps were at Bridgeport, on the Tennessee, about thirty miles from Chattanooga, which was the point at which the military operations centred. Though the country between Nashville and the advanced line of the Union army was in military possession of the loyal forces, it was in a very disturbed condition. There were strong Union men there; but the rebels predominated, and the region was infested with Confederate cavalry and irresponsible guerillas. The military railroad, by which the army received its supplies, was necessarily guarded by troops through every mile of its course.

Having procured their horses, Somers and De Banyan proceeded by the railroad towards their destination. The destruction of a bridge, about twenty miles from Bridgeport, suspended the farther progress of the train, and our officers decided to accomplish the balance of the journey on horseback. Each of them had a servant, and an extra horse to meet the contingencies of the service.

" We shall not be able to find our way, I'm afraid," said Somers, as they rode along through a wild region.

" You forget that I am at home in this part of the country," replied the major.

" Are you?"

" I was born and raised not twenty miles from this spot, in the town of Winchester, over in that direction," he added, pointing to the north-west. "I know every foot of land about here; and I am indebted to that fact for my appointment on the general's staff."

"Then we shall not be likely to get lost."

"No; but the guerillas are as thick around here as raisins in a plum pudding. I suppose I should have an excellent opportunity to be hung if any of them should catch me."

"What did you come down here for, then?"

"It makes no difference to me. I rather enjoy the excitement of the danger; besides, I should like to help restore my state to her allegiance."

"It is almost night, major. I don't think it is prudent for us to beat about this region in the dark."

"It is safer to beat about than it is to lie down and go to sleep; but there is a house a couple of miles from here, where a Union man used to live. We will stop there if you like."

"I think we had better do so," replied Somers.

"Perhaps we had, especially as it looks very much like a storm."

They reached the house, which was the residence of the owner of a large plantation. It had been an elegant establishment before the war, but it looked like waste and ruin around it. The travellers stopped before the mansion. De Banyan dismounted, and throwing the bridle-rein to his servant, walked up to the front door.

## CHAPTER XVIII.

### THE GUERILLAS AT SUPPER.

DE BANYAN knocked at the door; but as no one answered his summons, he went in without further ceremony, Somers remaining on his horse to await the result of the interview. It was now quite dark; the wind howled savagely through the trees, and the rain began to fall in torrents.

"Bad night, massa," said Alick, as he drew his overcoat closer around him.

"Yes; but we expect to stop at this house to-night," replied the captain.

"De storm make you sick again, massa."

"No, I think not."

"Must be careful, massa cap'n. I reckon dey has de fever 'n' agur right smart in dis yere country."

"I don't know," replied Somers, carelessly; for he was thinking that his friend was absent a long time upon his mission.

He waited a quarter of an hour longer, and began to be impatient at De Banyan's long absence. He thought the major must be having a very pleasant interview with his old acquaintance, and had forgotten that his friend was out in the storm waiting for him. At last his patience was completely exhausted, and he had it in his heart to rebuke the thoughtlessness of his companion.

"Here, Alick, hold my horse," said Somers, as he dismounted. "The major has gone to sleep, and forgotten that we are waiting for him."

"Yes, massa; but dat ain't much like de major, to forget you," replied Alick, taking the rein.

"No, it is not; but I'll venture to say he is having a good time in the house."

Somers walked up to the front door, and knocked with his fist. As in the former instance, it brought no response; and he repeated the summons with the butt of his pistol, but with no better success than before. It was evident that the family were very deaf, or that they occupied the rear of the house, where the sound could not reach them. Following the example of De Banyan, he opened the door and entered. At the end of a long entry he saw a light through a crack, which he followed till it brought him to another door, at which he knocked.

"What do you want?" demanded a large, rough, uncouth-looking man, who presented himself at the door.

"Where is the gentleman that came in here half an hour ago?" asked Somers, rather impatiently.

"Haven't any room," replied the man, in a loud tone.

"I asked where the gentleman was who came into the house half an hour ago," repeated the captain.

"I'm deaf."

"I should think you were," said the inquirer, in a low tone; after which he uttered his question again at the top of his lungs.

"I don't know him," yelled the deaf man.

"He came into this house."

"Four o'clock in the morning," screamed the man.

"Have you seen any one come into this house?" shouted Somers.

"Blind in one ear, and deaf in one eye," returned the man, with a grin.

"Who lives here?"

"I do."

"What's your name?"

"Skinley."

"What are you?"

"None o' yer business."

"Do you live alone?"

"What's that ter you?"

"I want to see the man that came in here a while ago."

"Come in."

Somers did not like the looks of things at all; and if he had not been interested in De Banyan, he would have retired in disgust from the house: as it was, he entered the room. As he did so he heard the sounds of coarse revelry, which suddenly burst upon his ear from an apartment farther in the rear of the mansion.

"Mr. Skinley, I wish to see the gentleman who came in before me," said Somers, putting his hand on his pistol.

"Do yer?"

"I do."

"Well, yer needn't yell no more; there ain't none so deef as them that won't hear. You kin see him," replied the man, with a grin, which seemed to indicate that Somers had been made the victim of a practical joke.

"Where is he?"

"In yender," replied Skinley, pointing to the door of the room from which the sounds of revelry had come.

Somers had a great many doubts in regard to the situation. There was evidently a considerable body of men in the house.

"Mr. Skinley — "

"I ain't *Mister* Skinley. I told you what my name was. My name's Skinley."

"Well, Skinley."

"That sounds more like it, stranger. Now, what's your name?"

"Somers."

"What are you?"

"None of your business."

"Whar yer gwine?"

"What's that to you?"

"All right, stranger."

"Now, Skinley, who are those men in yonder?" asked Somers, good-natured in spite of the circumstances of doubt, and possibly peril, which surrounded him, as he pointed to the rear room.

"Friends of mine."

"How many are there?"

"Go in and count 'em. What yer want to know fur?"

"A man in these times don't generally have so many friends as you seem to have."

"I'm a good feller, Somers, and they all like me," replied Skinley, laughing heartily.

"You have one of my friends in there."

"How do yer know?"

"You said so."

"Well, Somers, a feller don't allus know who his friends is, in these times."

"But I know him; and, Skinley, would you be so kind as to call him out?"

"It can't be did," said the uncouth abomination of a man, very positively.

"Why not?"

"Whar d'yer larn yer manners? He's havin' a bout

o' whiskey with the boys; and I'd as soon think o' techin' a pant'er at his grub as a sodger at his whiskey."

"If you tell him Somers is here, he will not take offence."

"Yes, he will. Them's good fellers. Go in and jine 'em," said Skinley, throwing the door wide open.

Seated around a long table, on which there was still a plentiful supply of bacon and corn dodgers, and a great many bottles, were about twenty of the roughest looking fellows the staff officer had ever laid eyes upon. At the end of the board was De Banyan, apparently as happy and contented as the rest of the party. Somers had no difficulty in promptly arriving at the conclusion that the men were guerillas. They had evidently drank all the whiskey that was good for them.

"Come in, Somers," shouted the major, uproariously. "Come in, and we will make room for you. My friend Somers," he added, turning to his wild companions.

"Come in, Somers," said half a dozen of the guerillas.

"Hand him the whiskey," put in one, who sat at the farther end of the table.

"You'll have to excuse him, boys," interposed De Banyan. "He never drinks whiskey; it don't agree with him. Have you any French brandy?"

"Not a drop."

The major knew they had not; he was aware that

Somers would fight the whole crowd rather than take a glass of liquor of any kind.

Somers was bewildered by the scene before him; but he readily understood that his friend was compromising with unfavorable circumstances, and he did what he could to help the illusion, though he did not know what De Banyan had said or done to create such remarkably good fellowship between himself and such wretched outlaws. He sat down at the table and ate heartily of the bacon and bread, which were very acceptable, for our travellers had eaten nothing since breakfast.

"Here's to the health of Jeff Davis!" said the man at the opposite end of the table, who appeared to be the commander of the squad. "All up."

The guerillas rose to their feet, De Banyan with them, with a glass in his hand.

"All up!" exclaimed the major, heartily.

Somers rose then, with a glass of water in his hand, which a black woman in attendance had brought him; but he had no more intention of drinking the health of Jeff Davis, even in a glass of water, than he had of supporting the arch rebel with his sword.

"President Davis," said the leader.

"President — Lincoln," added the major, dropping his voice as he uttered the last word.

"President — Lincoln," repeated Somers, in the same manner.

"One more!" shouted the commander of the squad, as he filled his glass again; and his example was followed by all present. "Here's confusion to the Yankees!"

"Confusion to the Yankees!" repeated the other guerillas.

"Confusion to the — rebels!" said De Banyan and Somers, using the same tactics as before.

The guerillas, as if satisfied that they had firmly established Jeff Davis on his throne, and hurled confusion among the Yankees, rose from the table. Their leader came over and took De Banyan by the hand.

"What did you say your name was?" asked he.

"De Banyan," replied the other.

"And you are going to join Wheeler's cavalry?"

"That's what's the matter," answered the major, who readily adapted himself to the manners of his new friends.

"Can't we make it worth your while to stay with us?" continued the chief. "You are a good fellow, and look as though you could fight."

"Wheeler expects me, and I don't wish to disappoint him. I'm going on his staff."

"There is something up to-night," said the chief, confidentially; "and you may make your fortune in a few days."

"I don't object to that."

"I'll tell you about it, if you like."

"I don't object."

"I don't know as I will, either; it would hardly be prudent for me to do so. You may be one of those shrewd Yankees, after all. You know you wear Yankee colors," added the chief, doubtfully.

"I tell you I was born in Winchester, not twenty miles from here; and I am no more a Yankee than you are," protested the major.

"I'll trust you," said the leader. "You can't spoil the job, if you don't help us. You are a tonguy fellow, and I want you more than I want the girl that promised to marry me when the war is over. I've got the smartest set of men that ever sat in a saddle. They are all Texans."

"I see they are," added De Banyan, glancing at the cutthroats who formed the squad.

"I've got the keenest scout on the lookout for me that you can find this side of the Rocky Mountains. He's a young fellow of eighteen, and goes inside the Yankee lines like a native. We go in for making money out of this thing, while we do a good job for the South."

"Of course," said De Banyan, carelessly.

"There's a pay-master coming down from Nashville, on one of these trains, with a heap of greenbacks to pay off the Yankee army. We want those greenbacks, and we shall have them too."

"If you can get them," suggested De Banyan.

"We can get them; and if you want your share of them, you have only to join my company. If you will, I'll tell you the rest."

"I'm yours," replied the major.

"And you?" asked the leader, turning to Somers, who had been listening eagerly to the conversation.

"I go with De Banyan."

"Good! Tippy — that's my scout — will come down in the train with the pay-master. The cars will stop at the broken bridge, and Tippy will come over here with his information; and all I have to do then will be to pounce on the escort, and pocket the greenbacks. What do you think of it?"

"It's a tip-top idea, and I'm with you."

"I expect Tippy will be here to-morrow."

"All right; I can help you about this business."

"You can; now, if you could step in and tell the pay-master you are a Yankee, and with that smooth tongue of yours prevent him from taking too much cavalry with him, you would earn your share of the money."

"I will do it."

"You can make a man believe anything."

"Very well; I will go at once."

"O, no; there is no need of going till Tippy comes with the news."

"I think I had better meet the train on the way."

"Not at all," said the guerilla, shaking his head.

"We never let our recruits go out till we know them better than I know you."

"You won't trust me?"

"Not yet."

"Very well," said De Banyan, easily. "My horse and servant are out in the storm now. I will take care of them."

"We will go with you;" and half a dozen of the villains followed De Banyan and Somers to the place where they had left the servants and the horses.

## CHAPTER XIX.

### TIPPY, THE SCOUT.

ON the way out of the house, De Banyan whispered a few words in the ear of Somers, while they were in the darkness of the entry. There was very great danger that things might get a little mixed; that Alick and the other servant might tell wrong stories about their respective masters.

"Tell Alick to say we are rebels," was the substance of the communication.

When they reached the spot where the horses had been left, Somers told his man what to say. It was fortunate that he did so promptly, for the guerilla leader, apparently suspecting something, suddenly became very officious, and kept close to the recruits. The horses were taken to the stable, where they were placed with the others, after which the party returned to the house, followed by the servants.

"What's your master's name?" demanded Captain Lynchman, the leader of the guerillas, of Alick.

"Captain Somers, sar," replied the faithful fellow.

"What is he captain of?"

"Dunno, sar."

"Where did you come from?"

"Up above, sar."

"Is your master a Union man?"

"I reckon he isn't, sar. He's a right smart reb'l, sar."

"Where are you going?"

"Dunno, sar."

"How long have you been in his service?"

"Much as a monf, sar."

The captain asked many other questions, but Alick gave prudent answers; he did not know much, and what he did know, he did not know certainly. De Banyan's man, taking his cue from his fellow-servant, answered in similar terms, and nothing was made out of either of them.

During the evening Somers learned, from various members of the band, that the guerillas were only a portion of an organized body, duly recognized by the Confederate government, engaged in partisan warfare. The talent and address of Major de Banyan had attracted the attention of the chief, who affected strategy rather than a bold and dashing policy. Captain Lynchman's perception was creditable to him, and if the major would have engaged in the foul business, he would undoubtedly have been an invaluable assistant.

Our travellers were regarded as members of the band, but really they were prisoners. They found no opportunity to interchange a word of counsel, or to take a single step for their future safety. Both of them were anxious to reach the headquarters of "Fighting Joe;" but the delay was not voluntary on their part. De Banyan had chosen between capture and compromise. He had presented, as he always did, a bold front, and disarmed suspicion in the beginning by his skill and address — had actually won the hearts of his new companions.

Captain Lynchman affected strategy, and while he carefully watched the recruits, he treated them with the utmost consideration. His future movements depended upon the information to be brought by Tippy, the scout. After the horses had been cared for, the guerillas retired for the night, some of them taking the beds, sofas, and divans, others stretching themselves on the floors; but there was no part of the house which was not occupied by them, and there was no opportunity for our travellers to "cut" their unpleasant associates during the night, as they had hoped and expected to do.

Early in the morning, Tippy, the scout, arrived. All the guerillas were at the stables, attending to the horses, when his coming was announced. The men were ordered to be ready to mount at an instant's notice; while Captain Lynchman hastened to the house, to receive the intelligence brought by the scout, who was eating his breakfast in the kitchen.

"De Banyan, I shall want you," said the leader; "your work will commence about this time. It will take the greenback train an hour or two to get ready for a start. Come with me."

"I am ready for anything," replied the major; and followed by Somers, he repaired to the house with the guerilla chief.

They entered by the front door, and taking possession of the drawing-room, the captain ordered Skinley, who seemed to be the commissary-general of the gang, to send the scout into the room.

"Skinley, you'll be deaf now," said Captain Lynchman.

"I reckon they ain't none so deef as them that won't hear," responded the Texan.

"Then you won't hear what Tippy has to say. Bring him in."

"Tippy's half starved, cap'n; they don't feed 'em much up among the Yanks."

"Let him eat, but tell him to be quick."

Skinley left the room; and then, for the first time, the captain noticed the presence of Somers, and told him to leave the room.

"He's my friend, Captain Lynchman; I have no secrets from him," interposed the major, with dignity.

"If you can't trust him, you can't trust me, and we will move on to the headquarters of Wheeler's cavalry."

"Just as you please, major," replied Lynchman; "but it is hardly regular."

"Nothing is very regular about these partisans. It is just as regular for him as for me. He is my right-hand man, and I can't do anything without him. I don't ask your confidence, and I don't want it. I am just as willing to go about my business as I am to stay with you."

"*I* am not willing, after telling you my plans."

"What did you tell them to me for, then?"

"Because I wanted you; and I did not expect to get you without offering big inducements. We shall divide three or four millions in greenbacks to-day, if we manage well. I believe in strategy in a case like this."

"So do I; and that is the very reason why I want Somers to know all about the matter."

While they were talking about it, Tippy, the scout, entered the room. He was a young man, with a bright eye and a manly form, and looked as though he was capable of doing all that had been claimed for him. He had eaten his morning meal very hastily; indeed, he had not finished it when he presented himself in the drawing-room, for his mouth was even now crammed full of corn cake, which he was trying to dispose of so that he could speak.

Tippy looked at Captain Lynchman first, crunching the food in his mouth in the most vigorous manner. From the leader, he glanced at Somers, who stood next to him. De Banyan had walked away to a window on the other side of the room, and as he turned to come back, the scout looked at him. Instantly his jaws ceased their movements, and he started back, apparently filled with astonishment. Somers looked at the major, who stood calmly at his side; but it was evident that he was not wholly unmoved by the appearance of Tippy.

"Well, what does all this mean?" demanded Captain Lynchman.

Somers again glanced at the major, and saw him give the scout a very slight, but energetic shake of the head, accompanied by a look which seemed to penetrate to the very soul of Tippy.

"Why don't you speak?" demanded Lynchman, impatiently.

Tippy improved this opportunity, still gazing intently on Major de Banyan, to swallow the food in his mouth. He finished this operation, and Lynchman waited for him to explain his singular conduct.

"Have you lost your tongue?" cried he, jumping out of his chair.

"I cannot speak," replied Tippy, exhibiting a great deal of emotion in his tones.

"Cannot speak! Do you know this man?"

"I do."

"Who is he?"

"Let him answer for himself. It is not for me to speak in his presence."

"What does all this mean?" said the guerilla leader, bewildered by the new aspect of affairs. "Who is this man, that you cannot speak in his presence?" he added, turning to the major.

"He is a bigger man than you or me," answered the scout, mysteriously.

"That may be, but I command here. Is he a traitor, or a Yankee?"

"No!" almost shouted the scout. "He belonged to Winchester once. He is a Tennesseean."

"Good!" exclaimed the captain, apparently much pleased with this confirmation of what the major had said of himself.

"Give your information, Tippy," added De Banyan, with an awful exhibition of dignity, as though he were the "big man" whom the scout had represented him to be.

"Not yet," said Lynchman. "I want to understand this matter a little better."

"We have been in Nashville together. We have worked together for years," interposed De Banyan.

"O, that's the idea — is it?" said the leader of the guerillas. "Then you are a scout yourself, Major de Banyan?"

"I have done a great deal of hard work in Virginia and in Tennessee. I have stood by the flag almost from the beginning," returned the major.

"Is this so, Tippy?"

"It is, Captain Lynchman. Whatever he says is right."

"Major, I am satisfied now," said the chief, extending his hand to De Banyan. "I wanted to repose implicit confidence in you before, but prudence forbade."

"We are losing time," said De Banyan.

"Now tell your story, Tippy," added Lynchman.

Somers was confounded by the events which had just transpired before him. He did not know what to make of them. His friend had a wonderful power over the scout, which he could not explain; but whatever occurred, he knew that De Banyan was a true man; that the recognition and devotion of the rebel scout to him were no evidences of infidelity. He could not understand, but he could trust the major.

"Shall I go on, sir?" said the scout, appealing to the major.

"Certainly; proceed," replied De Banyan.

Tippy's story was short and to the point. The paymaster with the greenbacks had arrived, and there was present a force of about a hundred cavalry to convoy him to his place of destination.

"A hundred!" exclaimed the captain, vexed at this information. "I shall want the rest of my men."

"You bet!" exclaimed a deep voice near the door, in low, emphatic tones, as though they had been used in soliloquy.

"Skinley!" cried the captain, angrily.

There was no reply, and Lynchman repeated the call half a dozen times, as loud as he could yell.

"D'ye call me, cap'n?" said the Texan, coming to the door, which was now discovered to be partially open.

"I did; you have been listening at the door."

"Fotch 'em as soon as I kin, cap'n," said the burly fellow, innocently.

"None of that with me," added Lynchman, angrily.

"Bet yer life they ain't, cap'n."

"Silence, you villain!" thundered the captain, taking a pistol from his belt.

"Take keer, cap'n!"

"Can't you hear, Skinley? If you can't, I'll open your ears."

"You told me to be deef, cap'n."

"I did; and you have been listening to all that has been said in this room."

"I was afeered you mought forget some on't, and mought wan't me to remound you of it."

"Come here."

"Here 'm I, cap'n."

"Do you know where the rest of our men are?"

"If I don't, nobody don't."

"Ride over there as fast as you can, and tell Sweetzer to meet me at Tantallon cross-roads at once, with all his force. Do you understand?"

"I kin hear now, cap'n."

"It will take you an hour to go, and another hour for Sweetzer to reach the cross-roads."

"How many men have you?" demanded De Banyan, in business-like tones.

"About a hundred," replied the captain. "We can make a sure thing of it, for we shall outnumber the Yankees, and choose our own ground besides."

"Where are they now?"

"At Raybold's, on the Salem road. I have driven them hard lately, and I gave them a few days to rest."

"I know the place. It is near the mountains."

"Just so. I believe in strategy, and I thought I should do better with twenty men than I should with over a hundred; but I calculated to take the greenbacks on the train."

"Your plans are good; but do you send only one man on such a message? Suppose he should fall from his horse, or be shot by a Yankee?"

"I can't spare but one, for I may have to do the job before the rest of my force arrives."

"Send Somers," suggested the major.

"What good would that do? He couldn't find my men?"

"Do you know where Raybold's is, Somers?" asked the major.

"Certainly I do — just by the mountains on the Salem road," replied Somers, who had given good attention to the conversation.

"Right; you will do," added the captain.

And Somers went with Skinley.

## CHAPTER XX.

### SKINLEY, THE TEXAN.

SOMERS readily understood that he was sent off by the major for a purpose; but De Banyan had no opportunity to explain his intention before he went. It was plain that a very important part in the plan for frustrating the object of the guerillas had been intrusted to him, but he had not a single word of instructions.

As Somers mounted his horse, he saw De Banyan and Tippy leave the estate and ride off in the direction of the railroad, and he doubted not that he had been sent to delay the pay-master, and assure him that the road to the army was perfectly safe. After the full and unequivocal indorsement of Tippy, the major was fully established in the confidence of the guerilla, who unreservedly communicated to him his hopes and his expectations.

Somers joined Skinley, who was to be his companion in this morning ride. The "Texican," as he delighted to call himself, was a stout fellow, good-humored, and immensely fond of a joke. Lynchman appeared to repose great confidence in him; otherwise he would not have sent him upon his present duty. The ruffian was armed from head to foot with rifle, pistols, and a knife, and looked like a moving arsenal. He was a formidable person for a young man like Somers to deal with, and yet it was fully evident that he had been sent by the major to prevent the "Texican" from delivering his message.

The young officer did not like the duty, for there was apparently only one way in which he could discharge it; and that was, by deliberately shooting his ugly companion. All the carnage and death he had seen in the course of the war — and he had seen a great deal of them — had not impaired his respect for human life. He could not wantonly sacrifice even an enemy. He was with this man as his friend — in disguise, it was true; but the Texan trusted him — did not regard him as a foe. To turn upon him in the moment when he suspected no danger, looked cowardly; and his chivalrous soul revolted at the act. Ruffian, rebel, traitor, as this man was, he was one of God's creatures, made in his own image, and nothing but the severest necessity could justify the killing of him.

Thus he reasoned on the one hand; but on the other, this man was going to procure a force to shoot down the loyal soldiers of the Union; to rob the government of the money intended for the troops, upon whose earnings wives and children depended for their daily bread. But this was war — what the custom of civilized nations justified; while killing a man in cold blood was an act of treachery from which he could not but shrink. War had not debased him, for he still read his Bible, and still leaned for strength and guidance upon that arm which can lead and support all who confide in its almighty power.

Somers felt that he could not do this deed. It was too revolting, too barbarous; and yet it must be done, or others would bleed and die for his want of nerve. He could not settle the troublesome question, and he determined to defer the deed as long as he could without imperilling the safety of the pay-master and his escort.

"Well, youngster, you mought be sent out to keep me warm, I 'spose," said Skinley, as Somers rode up to his side, after he had carefully considered the mission upon which he had obviously been sent.

"Yes, if you are cold," replied Somers.

"I am cold, Somers. May be yer hain't got a bottle of whiskey in yer pocket — hain't yer?"

"I have not; I never use it."

"So I heerd the major say; but hain't yer got nothin' stowed away about yer — any brandy, or sich like?"

"I have not."

"Well, Somers, I tell yer what it is, Somers, it was a great mistake comin' off without no whiskey, Somers."

"I don't think so."

"Don't yer, Somers?"

"I can get along very well without it."

"May be you can, Somers; but I can't. I feed on whiskey, Somers; and I could no more go to Raybold's without sunthin' to drink than I could go afoot on hossback, or go hossback afoot; 'n' I take it, Somers, that can't be did."

"But you will have to go without it, if you have none."

"No, I won't—you bet!" exclaimed Skinley. "Thar's a Union house over here a good piece. They allus has whiskey and bacon when we poor fellers has to thust fur meat and hunger fur liquor. The old man, I cal'late, is a fust cousin of some gin'ral, or some of them fellers in Richmond, fur he's got some sort o' paper. I'm gwine to git a drink when we git thar—bet yer life."

"But if they have a safe-conduct, you can't compel them to give you anything. They will show you the paper," replied Somers.

"Let 'em show it, Somers; I can't read it," chuckled the Texan.

"Why not?"

"Well, Somers, I ain't up to print, say nothin' of writin'. If they make any muss about it, I kin tell 'em it was all a mistake—don't yer see, Somers? May be I mought be deef too, Somers."

"Perhaps they will read it to you."

"Then I'm deef, sartin."

"Very likely they will give you what you want, if you ask them civilly."

"No, they won't, Somers. They hate us wuss'n pizen; but I hate them wuss'n they hate me."

"What have they done?"

"They hain't done nothin', and that's what I hate 'em fur. The Yanks won't tech 'em, and we can't tech 'em, Somers. It stands to reason, Somers, sech folks ought to be hated."

Somers decided not to discuss this question, and he had dropped a few paces behind his companion to avoid his slang, when Skinley exhibited a disposition to be sociable, and insisted that the road was wide enough for them to ride abreast. The young officer did not want to quarrel with the ruffian, and he complied with his request.

"Thar's a pooty gal over to Callicot's, Somers," added he, with a coarse grin. "P'rhaps you'll think more of that than yer do of the whiskey."

"Is she a Union girl?" asked Somers — more because he felt compelled to speak than because he felt any interest in the new subject.

"In course she are."

"You don't intend to meddle with her, I hope."

"What makes yer hope that?" demanded Skinley, sourly.

"Are you a soldier, Skinley?"

19

"You bet!"

"A true soldier always respects a woman, whether she be friend or foe."

"Somers, your idees is a little too fine cut fur me," snarled the Texan.

"Have you a mother?"

"Not's I knows on. She gin me the slip when I wan't knee high to a chaw terbaker."

"Is she dead?"

"I cal'late she is."

"Have you no sister?"

"May be I hev'. See here, Somers, you kin draw yer charge on that. Yer mought be a preacher, or sich like; but don't yer draw that string on me."

"Very well; I have nothing to say, only that, if you propose to insult a woman, I am your enemy."

"Be you?"

Skinley took a pistol from his belt, and deliberately cocked and pointed it at Somers, to whom the act seemed to reveal his companion in a new light. It was naturally to be supposed that a man who carried such an armory of weapons on his person was a dangerous fellow; but from this moment Somers looked upon him as a bully. He had given the ruffian no cause of offence for which he could resort to desperate measures.

"If you insult a woman, I am," replied Somers, quietly drawing a large navy revolver which he carried in his belt.

"Put up your shooter, Somers," said Skinley, with a sickly laugh, as he lowered his pistol.

"I am not quite ready to put it up," replied Somers, sternly; for he had made up his mind that the time to execute the task imposed upon him had come. "When a man draws a pistol upon me, he insults me."

"I only did it to see what sort of stuff you mought be made of, Somers — that's all," answered Skinley.

"I am not satisfied with that explanation. I would like to know what sort of stuff you 'mought' be made of now," said Somers, imitating the speech of his companion.

"I'm a Texican. I was born in the woods, nussed on hickory nuts, and turned out to paster in a cane-brake. When I kim of age I fed on gunpowder, and druv' four alligators, four in hand, hitched to a sulky. That's what's the matter. Don't you know now what sort of stuff I mought be made of?"

"Slang and brag, I should say, were the principal ingredients in your composition. You have insulted me."

"I ax yer pardon; put up yer shooter."

Somers did so, but very reluctantly. It was only postponing his mission; though the discovery that his companion was a coward at heart, in spite of his words, and in spite of the liberal display of arms about him, led him to hope that he might dispose of him in some better way than shooting him.

"I ax yer pardon; that's what a Texican does when he finds he mought be in the wrong."

"Very well. Now, if we can't talk without quarrelling, I will keep a little in the rear."

"Jest as you say, Somers."

They rode along in silence for a time, till they reached a house much superior to most of those they had seen on the road, at which Skinley halted.

"I'm sufferin' for my bitters, Somers," said the Texan, as he reined in his steed.

"Is this the house of the Union man?"

"Bet yer life 'tis. I only want a little drop of whiskey," replied Skinley, as he rode up the lane by the house, followed by his companion. "I won't stop only a second."

The guerilla dismounted, and throwing the bridle rein of his horse over a post, he entered without the ceremony of knocking. When he had gone in, Somers rode forward till he came to the windows of the house, for he was fearful that the conduct of the Texan would not be conciliatory, and he was disposed to defend the Union people within, even at the peril of his life.

Skinley was absent some time — longer than a due regard for the urgency of his mission would have tolerated; but Somers was in no hurry to reach Raybold's himself, and was not impatient on account of the delay. It was evident that the wretch had not readily procured his dram; and his companion feared that he might resort to violence in enforcing his demand. The delay indicated trouble within the house, and Somers dismounted. Fastening his horse to a gate, he walked towards the entrance. He was not one moment too soon, for before he could reach the door, he heard a piercing scream uttered by a female. He rushed in with his revolver in his hand.

"Don't yell," said Skinley, as he entered. "I only want yer to bring on the whiskey. I'm so deef I can't hear yer, if yer do yell."

Somers stopped at the door of the room where the parties were; for, indignant as he was, he was always prudent. He cocked the pistol, and took a survey of the situation.

"I tell you there is not a drop of whiskey in the house, and has not been for two years," replied the female, who was a young and well-dressed lady, and whose personal attractions fully justified the Texan's commendation of them.

"Yer mought tell that to a dead alligator, and he'd scretch yer eyes out fur't," added the ruffian.

"I have told you the truth; there is not a drop of liquor of any kind in the house."

"'Tain't so; all our boys knows you keeps whiskey by the hogshead. Now fotch on the liquor, my darlin';" and as he spoke, he grasped the lady by the arm.

She evidently regarded his touch as pollution, and again screamed lustily.

"See here; don't be so techy. I ain't gwine ter hurt yer."

"Father!" cried the terrified girl, shrinking from the wretch.

Somers would have fired, but he feared the report and the death of the ruffian before her face would be too great a shock for the lady. She was frightened, but she seemed to have perfect control of herself.

"Say, doxy, won't yer fotch on the whiskey?" continued Skinley; and again he attempted to seize the arm of the lady, who fled before him.

"Father!" screamed she again.

Somers stepped into the room; at the same instant an elderly gentleman rushed in by a door on the opposite side of the apartment.

## CHAPTER XXI.

#### THE HOUSE OF THE UNION MAN.

THE gentleman who entered the room from the other side was evidently Mr. Callicot, the father of the lady, and the Union man of whom the guerilla had spoken. He was unarmed, but there was a rifle hanging against the wall, after the manner of the South and West. The old gentleman was out of breath from hurry and excitement, and was hardly in condition to confront the ruffian, who had been bold enough in the presence of a timid woman.

"What do you want here?" demanded Mr. Callicot, in an excited tone.

"Nothin', squire, but a drink of whiskey," replied the Texan, glancing first at Somers, and then at the old man.

"There is not a drop of whiskey in my house, and has not been for years," answered Mr. Callicot.

"I'm a Texican, squire, and yer can't cheat me. I was born in the woods, and I kin smell whiskey nine mile off."

"I have told you the truth."

"No, yer hain't. Fotch on your whiskey, squire," added Skinley, taking one of his pistols from his belt.

"I have a safe-conduct from the general of this department," said the old man. "Here it is."

"I can't read it, stranger. Don't want ter read it, nuther."

"Perhaps you will read it," said Mr. Callicot, walking across the room, and handing it to Somers.

"Don't yer tech it, Somers," said the Texan, angrily.

Somers took the paper, glanced at it, and handed it back to the owner.

"Are you satisfied?" asked the old man.

"I am."

"That ain't handsome, Somers. Bekase you don't drink whiskey, it's onreasonable that you should spile my drink. But I'm gwine to hev my liquor. Now, squire, will yer fotch on the whiskey, or won't yer?"

"I would if I had any."

"But yer hev," said Skinley, raising his pistol; and before Somers could realize that he intended to fire, he discharged the piece at Mr. Callicot.

"O, my father!" screamed his daughter, rushing towards him.

"What do you mean, you villain?" cried Somers, elevating his pistol, and instantly firing.

"See here, Somers; that ain't handsome," replied Skinley. "I didn't tech you."

In the smoke that filled the room Somers had missed his aim, and the Texan was now entirely concealed from him.

"Leave the house!" shouted Somers.

"Not till I git my whiskey, if I knows it. I hain't killed the old man; didn't mean to kill him; only skeer him a little. May be you mought be willing to fotch on the whiskey now, squire."

"I have none, as I told you before," replied Mr. Callicot, who, finding he was not wounded, had, under cover of smoke, taken down the rifle from the beckets on the wall. "Now you will leave my house."

"Come, squire, don't be techy, but fotch on the whiskey," said Skinley, evidently not pleased with the new aspect of affairs.

"Leave my house!" replied the old man, with dignity.

Skinley, finding that it was of no use to argue the point, slowly backed out at the door by which he had entered.

"Shoot him, Somers," said he.

"You deserve to be shot yourself for this outrage," added Somers, indignantly.

"That ain't handsome, Somers. But we can't stop no longer," continued the Texan, as he left the house, and walked towards his horse.

"Begone, or you are a dead man," said Mr. Callicot to Somers, who still remained in the room.

"You mistake me, sir," returned Somers; "I am a friend, and not an enemy."

"Begone, or you shall die!" repeated the old man, now roused to the highest pitch of indignation. "You fired at me as well as the other ruffian."

"I fired at him."

At this moment the door by which the owner of the house had first entered was thrown wide open, and Somers discovered Skinley, who had gone round the house, and come in by another entrance. The wretch instantly raised his rifle, and fired. The old man dropped heavily on the floor, and his daughter uttered a scream of agony, as she threw herself on his body.

"That's the way a Texican settles yer hash!" shouted Skinley.

Somers, who had returned the pistol to his belt, drew it again, and fired in the direction of the door, though the smoke prevented him from seeing the form of Skinley. The guerilla rushed out of the house, and disappeared. Somers followed him, determined not to be balked this time. Unfortunately, he turned to the left, while the Texan went to the right; and when he had passed around the house to the lane, he discovered the scoundrel, already mounted, and spurring his horse away from the scene.

Somers sprang into his saddle, and started in pursuit. The hour had come to avenge the old man, and to

Skinley the Texan.
Page 227.

discharge the duty imposed upon him, now made easy by the wretch's crime. He urged forward his good horse to the utmost of his speed, and gained rapidly upon him. Skinley, who could insult a woman, and shoot an old man, had a wholesome fear of his pursuer; but when he found that Somers was gaining upon him, he unslung his rifle, and while his horse was at full speed, turned and fired at his late companion. The bullet did not come near Somers, who still urged on his steed.

Skinley, for some reason of his own, perhaps for the purpose of putting into operation some method of dodging his pursuer which he had learned in fighting Indians, or lassoing cattle, now turned into an open field. Whatever might have been the merits of the scheme under ordinary circumstances, it was fatal to him in the present instance; for, while the Texan was proceeding in a direction at right angles with the road, Somers dashed into the field, and cut him off, by taking the diagonal of the square, while Skinley was following the side. Perhaps he had not noticed a piece of low ground, partially covered with water, which compelled him to give Somers this advantage.

"'Tain't handsome, Somers; I didn't tech you!" yelled Skinley, when he perceived that he had lost the game.

Somers elevated his revolver, and, taking careful aim, fired. The wretch threw up his arms, sprang upward in his saddle, and dropped to the ground, while his horse dashed on at increased speed, when relieved of his heavy burden.

"My work is done," said Somers, as he drew in his panting steed.

Turning his horse, he rode slowly back to the spot where Skinley had fallen. Dismounting, he bent over the body to ascertain the result of his shot. The ball had struck the Texan in the side, and had evidently passed through his heart, for he was entirely dead. The old man was avenged; the plot of the guerillas, so far as it depended upon the arrival of Sweetzer and his force, was defeated.

Somers took from the corpse of the guerilla a rifle, three pistols, and a long knife. There was something projecting from the breast pocket of his coat which looked like a bundle of papers; and the young officer, ever intent upon procuring information, drew it forth. He was not mistaken; it was a bundle of papers, and among others there was a note from Captain Lynchman to Lieutenant Sweetzer; but it was only the order for him to proceed forthwith to Tantallon cross-roads. Inasmuch as Skinley was not "up to print," much less to writing, the remainder of the papers could have no connection with the bearer; but Somers was too much impressed by the proximity of the dead man, and by the necessity of prudence in his present condition, to examine them, and he put them in his pocket for future inspection.

Slinging the rifle upon his back, and placing the other weapons in his belt, he mounted his horse. As he was about to depart, the animal which had been ridden by Skinley came walking leisurely up the field, as if in search of his lost burden. When he saw Somers, he went up to him, and suffered himself to be captured. He was a docile creature, and had been well trained by his late master. Leading the horse, he returned to the house of Mr. Callicot, to ascertain the fate of that gentleman, and report the result of the pursuit.

He found the house in commotion. The few servants which the Union man had been able to retain were bustling about the house, but, as is apt to be the case in a panic, doing absolutely nothing. Somers gave the horses into the keeping of an old negro man, and having deposited the guerilla's weapons in the back room, entered the house. He found, by the direction which the servants took, where the dead or wounded man lay; for he had not waited to learn his fate before he went in pursuit of the wretch who had done the deed.

He entered the apartment, and was glad to find that his worst fears had not been realized. Mr. Callicot was not dead, but he appeared to be severely wounded. His eyes were open, and he was gazing, with a languid look of affection, at his daughter, who was bending over the bed.

"There's one of them," he faintly articulated, as Somers entered the room.

"I am not one of them, Mr. Callicot; on the contrary, I am an officer of the Union army, on the staff of the major general commanding the eleventh and twelfth corps."

"Impossible!" groaned the sufferer.

"More than this, I have shot the villain who fired at you," continued Somers.

"He certainly took no part with the other man, father," interposed the daughter; "and I heard him order his companion to leave the house."

"If you are still in doubt, you will find the villain's horse in your stable, and all his weapons in your back room."

"Go and see, Sophia," said the old man; "for we know not whom to trust."

Somers conducted the lady to the back room, and exhibited the weapons; then to the stable, where the negro had taken the horse.

"If you are not satisfied, Miss Callicot, you may send one of your servants to a field on the left of the road, about half a mile from here, and he will find the body of the guerilla, — for such he was."

"I am satisfied, sir; for I noticed the horse when the

man rode into the yard," replied the lady. "Why did you not protect us?"

"I fired at the scoundrel a moment after he discharged his pistol at your father the first time; but the smoke in the room spoiled my aim, and I missed him. I also fired at him when your father fell, as you must have noticed."

"I heard two shots, but I did not know who fired them."

"I supposed he had gone when he left the house; but it seems he went round, and entered again by another door. I did not think the ruffian was base enough to kill an old man like your father, or I would have shot him in the first place. I did not wish to do so in your presence."

"I wish you had."

"Is your father badly wounded?"

"I don't know how bad it is; he was struck in the shoulder. I have trembled every day for fear of these guerillas; but when they come with an officer, my father's paper always saves us from harm."

"Have you sent for a surgeon?" asked Somers.

"We have no horse at home, and the surgeon lives five miles from us."

"Take the dead man's horse."

"Thank you; I will send a man at once," replied Miss Callicot.

A boy was immediately despatched on Skinley's horse for a doctor, and Somers went with the lady to the room of her father. The young officer examined the wound, and ventured to assure the sufferer that it was not a dangerous one. When wounded himself, he had seen the surgeons operate, and he had some idea of the methods employed. The old man was bleeding freely; and by changing his position on the bed, and by pressing a napkin around the wound, he checked the flow of blood.

It was three hours before the surgeon arrived. He was a personal friend of the Union man, and came with all haste as soon as the boy found him. The doctor came, but the messenger did not return; and Somers concluded that the horse had been seen and recognized by some of the guerillas. The young officer was greatly perplexed in regard to his future movements; and though Miss Callicot offered, and pressed upon him, the hospitalities of the house, he decided to depart as soon as the doctor had assured him that the wound was not dangerous. Leaving at the house the guerilla's weapons, which he advised the lady to conceal, he mounted his horse, and rode away; but what to do, or where to go, he was at a loss to determine. All he wanted now was, to find De Banyan, and hasten to the headquarters of his general.

The attack upon the pay-master's escort was to be made at Tantallon cross-roads, or in that direction; but it was not prudent for him to be seen near that locality, after what had happened, and he decided to return to the nearest military post on the railroad. After riding a couple of miles, as he turned a bend in the road, on the verge of a wood, he suddenly came upon Lynchman's force, which had halted there.

20*

## CHAPTER XXII.

#### THE GREENBACK TRAIN.

THE guerillas and their horses stood so still in the road that Somers had not suspected their presence. His first impulse was to wheel his horse, and flee with all speed from this dangerous ground. The fact that the negro boy, who had been sent for the doctor, had not returned, was pretty good evidence that he had been captured by the guerillas; and their presence in this place fully confirmed his fears.

To turn and run away would be sure to bring a volley from their carbines upon him, and to advance was to throw himself into the very jaws of the lion; but, on the whole, he decided that it was less perilous to go forward, and he continued on his way, as though no shock had come over him. The negro who had been captured had probably told his story, and it would be a very difficult matter to reconcile the conflicting statements that must ensue.

"Why are you here, Somers?" demanded Captain Lynchman, in an excited tone.

"Yankee cavalry," replied Somers, glancing suspiciously behind him.

"Where?"

"I don't know where they are now. Skinley was shot by a Yankee and killed."

"This is bad business," said Lynchman.

"No, it isn't; it is all the better for us," said De Banyan, stepping forward to the rescue.

"Perhaps it is, but I don't see it," added the captain; and truly it must have been rather difficult for him to see.

"You are duller than usual, captain," continued De Banyan, with his easy assurance. "You believe in strategy, and look troubled at a difficulty like this?"

"Did you give Skinley's horse to that nigger?" demanded Lynchman.

"Bah!" exclaimed De Banyan, with hearty disgust. "What matter whether he did or not? Are you going to settle a case of that sort now? I tell you it is all right."

"What shall we do?"

"Do?" sneered the major. "We will capture the pay-master at Tantallon cross-roads, as we intended. We are not going to be thrown off the track by a little accident of this kind."

"Of course not," replied the guerilla, catching the inspiration of his apparently bolder companion.

"Leave these Yankees to me," continued De Banyan. "I will have them ten miles from here within two hours."

"Good!" murmured several of the guerillas.

"The greenback train has been delayed, and we shall have time to bring up Sweetzer yet. I want two men to go with me. I will take Tippy and Somers."

"What do you want of them?" demanded Lynchman.

"Somers shall go to Raybold's for our fellows there, and Tippy shall return to inform you when to come forward. If you should be seen, it would spoil the whole thing."

The guerilla chief consented to this plan; and De Banyan, followed by Somers and Tippy, rode off at full gallop. The major did not seem to be conscious that he had very cleverly performed the part he had assumed in the drama. He looked just as determined as though he intended to carry out the programme assigned to him by Lynchman.

"What are you going to do, major?" asked Somers, when they had ridden about half a mile.

"The infernal cutthroats!" exclaimed he, savagely. "I'm going to capture the whole crowd."

"But you have no force."

"I'll have one. Tippy!" said he, with energy.

"Sir," replied the scout, with the utmost deference and respect.

"Understand my purpose. I am going to the stockade where the pay-master and his escort are, and where I requested him to remain until he heard from me."

"Have you seen him?" asked Somers.

"I have; he has sent to the next post for more men. They must have reached him by this time. Now, Somers, if we are smart, we will report to the general before night with the pay-master, and these guerillas as prisoners. We have got things now where we can have it our own way, and it will be our fault if we don't bag the whole squad."

"If the pay-master has a hundred men, we can take them at once," said Somers.

"I propose to haul in the whole company — those at Raybold's as well as those with Lynchman. We have no time to lose," continued the major, with increased energy. "Somers, you must go to Raybold's, and deliver the message given you by the captain."

"I'm willing," replied Somers, taking from his pocket the papers he had removed from the body of Skinley. "I have the captain's written order in my hand."

"Good! Kill your horse, if necessary; but don't lose an instant of time. Away with you!"

"But I don't know the road."

De Banyan instructed him very carefully in regard to his route.

"When you have delivered the order, look out for

yourself," he added, as Somers put spurs to his willing horse, and dashed away to execute his important mission.

"Now, Tippy, in one hour go and tell Lynchman that the road is open for him," added De Banyan, as he took the hand of the young scout, which he pressed with warmth. "Boy, be true to your country and your flag from this time henceforth and forever!"

"I will, I will!" exclaimed Tippy, with deep feeling, as he wiped away the tears, which, for some unexplained reason, filled his eyes.

De Banyan, apparently as deeply moved as the young man, galloped away at a furious pace. Beyond the wood he turned to the left, crossing the creek and the railroad, till he reached another road. This point was Tantallon cross-roads; and here he turned to the left again, and was now moving directly towards the stockade in which he had left the pay-master, and where he arrived in an hour from the time he started. In fifteen minutes more a squadron of cavalry, collected during the forenoon from the military posts in the vicinity, was moving down towards the cross-roads.

When the force arrived at its destination, one half of it was posted in a secure place by the railroad, where it could not be seen by the guerillas as they advanced to the rendezvous, and the other half in the vicinity of the cross-roads. Quite as soon as they were expected the little troop of Lynchman crossed the railroad, and moved cautiously towards the point at which they expected to meet the "greenback train." But no sooner had they passed the railroad, than the force in their rear took the road and cut off their retreat, while that in front advanced upon them. For a moment there was a clash of arms; but the guerillas were borne under and captured by the cavalry without the loss of a man, and almost without a scratch on either side.

The prisoners were conducted to a safe place, and the cavalry again disposed for the reception of the larger force expected from Raybold's. The guerillas were intensely astonished at the sudden and unexpected result of the enterprise. Captain Lynchman, who believed in strategy, looked exceedingly foolish and disconsolate. When the prisoners were halted in a secure position he happened to see De Banyan.

"How's this?" said he, appealing to the energetic major.

"How's what?" asked De Banyan, with admirable simplicity.

"You have made a blunder somewhere," added Lynchman, sheepishly.

"Not at all. Everything has come out just as I intended it should."

"Then you are a traitor."

"On the contrary, I am a true Union man. I go for the Union first, and Tennessee next."

"Traitor!" growled the guerilla.

"See here, my man; you believe in strategy — don't you?"

"I do."

"So do I," replied De Banyan. "I think you have got strategy enough to last you till the end of the war."

"You deceived me, then," added Lynchman, bitterly.

"Deceived you!" sneered the major. "Did you think I would throw myself into your arms, and let you butcher me at your own pleasure. I know what you guerillas are — gorillas, I had better say. Deceived you! I shouldn't want a more stupid fellow than you are to work upon. You have played into my hand all the way through."

"What is to be done with us?" asked the discomfited chief, tamely.

"I don't know. We shall march you to headquarters; but as a man of your importance ought to have a bigger escort than this, we shall add the rest of your gang to the train."

De Banyan walked away, mounted his horse, and rode down to the cross-roads again, where the greater battle was soon to be fought. Tippy, the scout, who had disengaged himself from his companions at the beginning of the affray, was directed to keep at a distance from the strife.

Somers delivered his message to Sweetzer, and the

guerillas immediately leaped into their saddles. The note from Lynchman relieved the bearer from all suspicion, and the lieutenant only questioned him in regard to the nature of the operations in which his force was to engage. Somers answered as suited himself; and, finding that no further notice was taken of him, the officers and men being busily occupied in preparing for their excursion, he contrived to detach himself from their company. Gaining the highway, he rode at a leisure gait till he was out of their sight, when he quickened his pace, and reached the cross-roads in advance of the guerillas. He was warmly welcomed by De Banyan; but there was no time yet for long stories, though both of them had much to say.

Sweetzer and his men crossed the railroad without a suspicion that they were plunging into a fatal trap, till they heard the clatter of horses' feet behind. The cavalry in the rear, which was to open the battle, dashed upon the guerillas with a round of Union cheers. But the rebels were desperate fellows. They had been plundering, murdering, and destroying, without mercy, and the fear of a righteous retribution upon their heads nerved them to the most determined action, and they fought like demons.

They were hardly engaged before the cavalry in front rushed with headlong speed upon the entrapped foe. It was such an opportunity as the policy of the partisans seldom permitted them to enjoy; and the Union soldiers, with a hearty relish for the work, went into the fight with an enthusiasm which could result only in speedy victory. Then ensued a brief but tremendous conflict, in which the guerillas were thoroughly and completely routed. There was an awful cutting and slashing for a few minutes. The rebels were utterly demolished; they broke, and attempted to flee from the scene of wrath; but not many of them escaped.

"The work is done," said De Banyan, as he joined Somers at the close of the conflict.

"And well done," added Somers, as he returned his sword to its scabbard. "I think the general will be willing to excuse our delay in reporting."

The wounded were sent back to the military post, the prisoners secured, and the "greenback train" took up its line of march for the army.

On the way, De Banyan, Somers, and Tippy kept together. It was the first time the staff officers had found an opportunity to communicate in regard to the past. Somers knew but little of what his friend had done; but he opened the way for an explanation by relating his own adventures with Skinley.

"I supposed you would shoot him the moment you got him out of sight of his cutthroat companions," said the major.

"I couldn't shoot him down in cold blood. I intended

to use a little strategy, when the right time came," replied Somers.

"You are too sentimental by half. If he had been a soldier and a decent man, you might have hesitated. He was nothing but a cold-blooded wretch, a cutthroat; you ought to have shot him without winking twice. I would have done it."

"I couldn't do it. But, De Banyan, what have you been doing?"

The major minutely detailed his operations during the morning. He had been to the pay-master, proved that he was a Union man, on the staff of a general, and exposed the plot of the guerillas. Returning to them, he had arrived just before the capture of the negro boy on the Skinley horse, and had contrived to make the fellow say what he desired, in part, and to neutralize what tended to inculpate Somers.

"One question, major," said Somers, when De Banyan finished: "Who is Tippy?"

"He is my son."

## CHAPTER XXIII.

#### THE BATTLE IN THE CLOUDS.

SOMERS had been greatly mystified by the singular conduct of Tippy, the scout, and quite as much so by that of De Banyan in connection with the young man. He remembered to have heard the major say, when they parted, after the eventful campaign before Richmond, that he had a son; and it now appeared that he had been in the rebel service, while his father was actively engaged on the other side.

Before the war Tippy had been the confidential friend and companion of his father to an extent to which parents seldom admit their sons. He was an only child, and between them there had been a bond of sympathy, which nothing but the total breaking up of all social relations could affect. The father had been compelled to enter the rebel army sorely against his will, and at the first opportunity had put himself on the right side. In doing so he had been separated from his family, hoping, however, to meet his wife and son again in a few months at farthest. He had been grievously disappointed in this respect, for the sweep of the Union army had not been so speedy and decided as he had anticipated; and he had been obliged, by the force of circumstances, to leave the West and go to the East.

During his absence his wife had died; and the son, inheriting the talent of his father, had taken service in the rebel ranks, where his ability as a scout was soon discovered. When he saw his father, he had no will of his own; whatever the parent was, he was. Like thousands of others who fought on the side of rebellion, he had no principle in the matter, and only went with the crowd. He was now happily restored to his devoted parent, and fully believed that whatever cause his father espoused must be the right one. The boy's middle name was Tipton, after a Tennessee politician, who happened to be in the ascendant at the time of his birth; and from this was derived the pet appellation by which he was known among the rebels and partisans.

Somers and Tippy were immediately the best of friends; and during the day, as they rode along, the young Tennessean asked a thousand questions about the North, about the home and the associations of his companion; and it is quite probable that he profited by the information imparted in the answers to the questions.

Before night, as De Banyan had promised, our travellers had the pleasure of reporting to "Fighting Joe," at Bridgeport, and of receiving a hearty welcome. They were warmly commended for the work they had done among the guerillas, who were the pest of the state, the continual annoyance of the army's communications, and a nuisance to friend and foe among the families of the region. The general conversed freely with De Banyan and Somers, and immediately assigned them to duty in their respective positions.

"Somers, my dear fellow, I greet you!" exclaimed Captain Barkwood, when they met.

"Thank you, captain," replied Somers, warmly grasping the proffered hand of the engineer.

"You are the only volunteer I have met who was fit to be a regular."

"Fortunately, I am one," added Somers, explaining his position.

"I congratulate you. I hear that you have been fighting guerillas."

"A little."

"I am sorry you have a taste for those small squabbles."

"I have not; I only go into them from necessity. But our fight with the guerillas was a splendid piece of strategy. I will tell you about it."

Somers told him, and the engineer was satisfied, though he declared that he was too much of a coward to have any relish for hand-to-hand encounters.

"Well, Captain Barkwood, how is the general?"

asked Somers, when the relative merits of brain and muscle had been duly discussed.

"The general! He is a diamond among precious stones," replied Barkwood, with enthusiasm. "If he gets a chance he will knock the backbone out of the rebel army in this quarter. By the way, Somers, I remember the general when he was in Mexico."

"Were you there?"

"I was."

"You don't look old enough."

"I'm forty. I remember him at Chapultepec."

"I was there," added De Banyan; "but I was a private."

"He fought like a tiger there, as he did everywhere, and went up like a rocket from second lieutenant to lieutenant colonel. He is what I call a positive man; he does his own thinking, which, unfortunately for him, perhaps, in some instances, does not agree with the thinking of others. He was with Pillow, Rains, and Ripley, who are all rebels now."

"But the general left the army."

"Yes, he is an active man; he couldn't stand the piping times of peace that followed the Mexican war, and, resigning his commission, went to California, where he became a farmer. This didn't agree very well with his constitution, and when a speck of war appeared in 1861, he hastened to Washington; not as an adventurer, mind you, but as a man who believed in the American Union. Somehow the men in authority seemed to have forgotten about his conduct in Mexico; and it may be that some of his positive opinions were remembered, and he did not readily procure service.

"Discouraged, and perhaps disgusted, with his ill success, he made up his mind to return to his farm on the Pacific. Before his intended departure he paid his respects to President Lincoln, to whom he made some comments on the battle of Bull Run, which induced the president to make him a brigadier. That was the luckiest thing for the general, and the luckiest thing for the country, that ever came out of an accident."

"That's so!" exclaimed De Banyan, with emphasis. "I've seen him in a great many fights; and I say he has no superior in the army."

"I'm not very fond of comparisons between generals; but I can say I like him better than any other," added Somers. "I wish generals were not so sensitive."

"Sensitive? My dear Somers, a man can no more be a great general without being sensitive, than he can be a parson without being pious."

"That may be; but I think that some of the military operations of the war have failed because the commanding general in charge of them was not fairly supported, owing to some of these squabbles about rank."

"That's true; but there's a great difference between

being sensitive, and failing to obey orders, in spirit as well as to the letter. 'Fighting Joe' never did and never will allow his sensitiveness to endanger for one moment the success of our arms," said the engineer, warmly. "He would fight under a corporal rather than lose the day, any time."

"I know that," answered Somers; "but I can't help feeling that if some generals had been less sensitive, our general would have been in command of a large army to-day."

"A positive man speaks what he thinks; and I doubt not 'Fighting Joe' has often offended his superiors by his candid criticisms. This may have affected his position, but it cannot rob him of the glory of the past. Whatever he does, and wherever he goes, I'm with him to the end," added the engineer.

"So am I," said De Banyan.

"There will be something done in this department very soon," continued Barkwood. "The heavy storms have rendered the roads almost impassable; and the provisions for the army in Chattanooga have to be conveyed in wagons about fifty miles. The first move will be to open the river and the railroad between this point and Chattanooga."

The engineer was correct in his supposition, for a few days later General Hazen's brigade descended the Tennessee in pontoon boats, intended for the erection of a bridge over the river at Brown's Ferry, running the rebel batteries in the night, and reaching their destination in safety. The Confederate force under General Bragg was posted on the south side of the river, holding the heights known as Raccoon Mountain, Lookout Mountain, and Missionary Ridge. Batteries had been planted on these heights, which swept the river and the valleys; and the operation of dislodging the enemy from their strongholds was a difficult and dangerous one.

A pontoon bridge nine hundred feet in length was built on the river at Brown's Ferry in five hours, a force having been first sent over the river, and a position captured and fortified to protect the operation. The eleventh and twelfth corps then moved out from Bridgeport, and completed the communication between that place and the pontoon bridge, thus effecting a junction with the army in Chattanooga. A steamboat, built by a company of engineers, and another captured from the enemy, conveyed provision, one above and the other below the pontoon bridge, to the beleaguered town. This vital question being settled, the place was fortified so that it could be held by a small force; and the main army then commenced the work of relieving East Tennessee from the presence of the rebels, which was fully accomplished in spite of the active movement of the enemy to prevent it.

Our volume is not a history, and we do not purpose to

narrate in detail the movements of the three armies, which had been united under General Grant. The rebels were whipped in every direction, foiled and defeated in all their plans, and the Union army continued on its march to Atlanta. "Fighting Joe" bore an important part in these operations, and was conspicuous at Lookout Mountain, Resaca, and before Atlanta. He was skilful and brave, energetic and devoted in this campaign, as he had been before. He was faithful to his duty, until, on the death of General McPherson, he was compelled to ask to be relieved. With this summary of the events at the seat of war in the South, we return to Captain Somers.

The general's command, having opened the communication with Chattanooga, marched up Lookout Valley. "Fighting Joe" was there for a purpose. The rugged steeps of the mountain bristled with rebel cannon, and his army was exposed to a sharp fire as it moved on its way. The general was in the midst of it, and assured the troops that the fire could not harm them. His conduct had the most inspiring effect upon the men.

When the head of the column approached the vicinity of the railroad bridge, near Wauhatchie, the rebel infantry opened upon it, being posted in a dense forest, where their number could not be determined. A brigade was thrown out to flank the position, upon which the enemy precipitately fled over the creek, burning the bridge behind them. The column moved on, and halted for the night in the valley.

At midnight General Geary's division was savagely attacked, and presently the gloom of the valley was lighted up by the flame of battle; cannon and musketry blazed from the summits of the mountain, but the men fought with the most determined zeal. The general was in his saddle, and his staff were hurled away like arrows from a bow, to strengthen the weak parts of the line. A brigade was despatched to the assistance of Geary, who was hard pressed; but the attack was promptly repelled.

Somers was then sent off with an order to the second brigade to storm the heights and carry them; and he was directed to accompany the force and report progress to the general. The hill was very steep and rugged, and in many places the rocks presented the appearance of palisades. It was covered with wood and underbrush, and it would not have been an easy thing to climb it with a guide in broad daylight; but the general had sent these intrepid fellows to scale its jagged steeps in the middle of the night. It was cloudy, and the moon shed an uncertain light on the scene.

To Somers there was a savor of home in the enterprise, for the thirty-third Massachusetts was one of the two regiments which formed the advance in this perilous movement; the other was the seventy-third Ohio, both numbering only four hundred men. On dashed the intrepid soldiers, climbing up the dangerous steeps, as though all of them had been mountaineers — on, till they penetrated the clouds, while the gloom was lighted up by the glare of the sheets of flame from two thousand rebel muskets. There in the clouds, at midnight, was fought and won this remarkable battle. The crests of the hills were carried at the point of the bayonet, and the gallant thirty-third left one third of its number killed and wounded on the ground; but the victory was complete, and Captain Somers hastened to report the result to the general.

22

## CHAPTER XXIV.

#### PEACH-TREE CREEK.

During the night all the rebels evacuated Lookout Mountain, and retreated upon the main army, posted at the eastward of them. The storming of the heights was part of the great battle of Chattanooga, directed by General Grant with the most consummate skill, and carried out by his subordinates with a zeal and energy which insured a great and decisive victory. Chattanooga was ours; East Tennessee was purged of the rebels who had been persecuting the devoted loyalists from the beginning of the war; and with these events substantially closed the campaign of 1863.

Our limited space compels us to pass over the time from this period to the July of the next year. Somers and De Banyan still held their positions on the staff of the general, spending the winter in the vicinity of Chattanooga. There were a great many letters passed between the young captain and his friends, and all of them from him were not directed to Pinchbrook.

Between himself and Lilian a most excellent understanding still subsisted.

In the reorganization of the army, which followed the well-deserved promotion of Grant to the rank of lieutenant general, "Fighting Joe" was placed in command of the twentieth corps; and in Sherman's bloody and decisive advance to Atlanta, he was one of the central figures in the picture. He was the idol of his corps, as he had been in the Army of the Potomac. His men loved and trusted him, and he never disappointed them. He was always in the thickest of the danger, to support and to cheer them.

Everything went wrong with the rebels. Johnston, beaten and flanked time and again, fell back, until Atlanta, the objective point of Sherman, was reached, where he was superseded by Hood, who was eminently a fighting man, and was expected to retrieve the failing fortunes of the Confederacy. On the 20th of July was fought the battle of Peach-Tree Creek, which was a desperate attempt on the part of the newly-appointed rebel commander to redeem the disasters of the past. The attack was made against a weak place in the line, where there was a large gap between the divisions of Geary and Williams.

Into this gap Hood hurled his compact column; who, inspired with a hope that their new leader would turn the tide of battle setting so strongly against the rebels, fought with unwonted desperation. They poured, in solid masses, through the open space, and fell upon the boys of the twentieth corps with fiendish valor. For a moment they shook — but "Fighting Joe" flashed before them like a meteor; his full tones were heard as buoyant as in the hour of victory, and the soldiers gathered themselves up under this potent inspiration, and bravely faced the impetuous foe. From both sides of the gap, into which the rebels had wedged themselves, deadly volleys of musketry were poured in upon them. They were mowed down like ripe grain before the scythe. They bit the dust in hundreds; but the survivors maintained the conflict.

Still the commander of the twentieth corps dashed along the line, and everywhere restored the breaking column. His voice was a charm on that day, and more than any other of the war in which he had been engaged, this was his battle; for, with his voice, his eye, and his commanding presence, he banished panic, and wrested victory from the arms of defeat. The assault was triumphantly repelled; and doubtless the rebels believed that the Fabian policy of Johnston was preferable to the bloody and bootless desperation of Hood.

The battle was won; and many and earnest were the congratulations exchanged among officers and soldiers after the bloody affair. De Banyan and Somers had been particularly active, not only in bearing orders, but in rallying the troops; and the general personally thanked them for their devotion: at the same time the aid-de-camp was directed to convey information of the result to a general whose position might be affected by it.

Somers rode off, but had gone only a short distance before his friend dashed up to his side, and pointed out to him a piece of woods on his route, where a squad of the enemy's cavalry had been seen, and entreated him to be exceedingly cautious.

"I'm always cautious, major," laughed Somers.

"I know you are, my boy; but you might not have known there was any danger in that quarter."

"I will avoid the woods, if I can."

"You can, by going over that low place at the right of the creek," added De Banyan. "I have a message to deliver in that direction myself."

They rode on, and parted a short distance from the creek. Somers proceeded to his destination, and having accomplished his mission, started on the return. When he reached the point nearest to the creek, his attention was attracted by a riderless horse, feeding on the shrubs that covered the ground. A nearer approach to the animal assured him it was De Banyan's horse; and his blood froze with fear as he considered the meaning of this circumstance. His friend had evidently been shot, and had fallen from his horse; but perhaps he was not dead, and Somers proceeded to search for the major.

As he rode forward, almost overcome by the suddenness of the shock which had fallen upon him, the sharp crack of a rifle roused him from his meditation, and a bullet whistled uncomfortably near his head. He drew his revolver, and discovered half a dozen rebels in front of him. Wheeling his horse on the instant, he attempted to escape in the opposite direction. This act drew upon him the fire of the party, and though he was not hit, his horse dropped upon the ground, shot through the head. As the faithful animal fell, the leg of the rider became entangled under his body, and he was held fast.

"How are you, Blueback?" said one of the rebels, as they rushed forward and seized him, disarming him before they released him from his uncomfortable position.

"How are you, Grayback?" replied Somers, calling his philosophy to his aid in this trying moment.

"Is yer health good, Yank?"

"First rate, I thank you, Reb," answered Somers, as he disengaged his foot from the stirrup beneath the horse. "How's yours?"

"I cal'late you are better ter keep than yer are to kill."

"That's a sensible idea on your part."

"May be it is. What yer got in your pockets, Yank?"

"Not much; the pay-master hasn't been round lately."

"Let's see."

"You rebs don't take greenbacks — do you?" asked Somers, as he pulled out his pocket-book.

"I bet we do — take anything we can get."

"Well, you won't get much out of me. There's my pocket-book; it's rather flat; an elephant stepped on it the other day."

There was about ten dollars in legal tender currency and fractional bills in the pocket-book, which the rebels thankfully accepted.

"What else yer got?" demanded the spokesman of the squad.

"What else do you want? When I meet a friend in distress, I like to do the handsome thing by him."

"I reckon we're in distress, and we'll take anything yer got to give. Got the time of day about yer?"

Somers gave up his silver watch.

"That's everything I have about me of any value," he added, hoping these sacrifices would satisfy the rapacity of his captors.

"Dunno, Yank; let's see," added the rebel, with a grin. "Turn out yer pockets."

Somers took from the breast pocket of his coat the Testament which his mother had given him, and which had been his constant companion in all his campaigns. It contained several pictures of the loved ones at home, including, of course, one of Lilian Ashford.

"You don't want this?" said he, as he pulled the Testament, wrapped up in oiled silk, from his pocket, and unrolled it before them.

"I cal'late you Yanks don't hev no use for this book," replied the spokesman, as he took the cherished gift.

"Won't you leave me that?" asked Somers. "My mother gave it to me, and it contains the photographs of my friends at home."

"Not if I knows it, Yank," replied the man, coarsely. "This is a warm day — ain't it, Yank?"

"Rather warm."

"May be that coat's too hot for yer?"

"I think I can endure it very well."

"I'm feered it will make yer sick if yer wear it any longer. Jest take it off, Yank. It was made for a better man 'n you be."

Somers complied, simply because resistance was vain.

"What number of boots do you wear, Yank?" continued the rebel, glancing at his prisoner's feet.

"Well, I generally wear two of them," replied Somers, facetiously.

"I reckon yer won't wear so many as that much longer. Don't yer think them boots would fit me?"

"I'm afraid they are too small for you," said Somers, disgusted with the conduct of his captors.

"I reckon they'll jest fit me."

"Come, Turkin, quit now. I'll be dog-on'd ef we

don't git captered ourselves, ef you keep on parlatin' with the carri'n any longer. Fotch him along, and we'll measure the boots bime-by."

As this was eminently prudent advice under the circumstances, Turkin decided to follow it. One of the party took the saddle and bridle from the dead animal, while another caught De Banyan's horse. The unfortunate event took place within fifty rods of the line of the twentieth corps, and near the spot where the recent battle had raged fiercest. The ground was directly in front of the army, and it was an unparalleled piece of impudence for the rebels to come so near on such an expedition. With the exception of the piece of woods, the ground was open, though Somers was captured behind a ridge, which hid the marauders from the view of the sentinels.

"Now, Yank, we'll march," said Turkin, who, though he wore no badge of his rank, appeared to be the sergeant or corporal commanding the squad. "Be you ready?"

"Well, no, I'm not ready; but as you fellows have such an insinuating way with you, I suppose I shall have to go," replied Somers, glancing in the direction of the Union line.

"You guessed about right that time, Yank. 'Tain't no use to look over yender. If yer don't walk right along, jest like a Christian, I'd jest as lief shoot yer as not."

"Don't trouble yourself, Reb; I'm with you. But I'm not much used to walking without boots, of late years, and if you take my boots I may make hard work of it."

"No, yer won't; if yer do, I'll save yer the trouble of walking any further."

"No trouble at all," added Somers, who, in spite of his apparently easy bearing, was in momentary fear of being shot by the ruffians in charge of him.

"What's yer name?" demanded Turkin, abruptly, as they moved towards the wood, beyond which flowed Peach-tree Creek.

"Thomas Somers."

"What d'yer b'long ter?"

"To the army."

"See here, Yank; I asked yer a civ'l question; if yer don't give me a civ'l answer, dog scotch me if I don't give yer pineapple soup for supper."

By pineapple soup Somers understood him to mean a minie ball, deducing this conclusion from the resemblance of this messenger of death to the fruit mentioned. The rebel seemed suddenly to have changed his humor, and the captive found that it was not safe to give indirect answers; so he told who and what he was in full, without any equivocation.

"Can you tell me what became of the owner of that horse?" said Somers, pointing to the animal, led by one of the rebels; but he did not venture to put the question to Turkin.

"May be I can; but may be I won't," replied the man, in surly tones.

"Was he killed?"

"If he was, he was; if he wasn't, he wasn't."

Somers could obtain no information on this subject, and he feared the worst.

## CHAPTER XXV.

### THE MONKEY AND THE CAT'S PAW.

NOTWITHSTANDING his own misfortunes, Somers could not help thinking of his friend De Banyan, whom he regarded as an elder brother. They had endured much suffering, and passed through many perils together, and the bond of union between them was very strong. The riderless horse indicated that he had been killed. The rebels had fired upon Somers before they summoned him to surrender, and probably a shot aimed at De Banyan had been more unfortunate. It was very sad for Somers to think of his noble companion, shot down by an unseen foe; but he could hardly cherish a hope that he was still alive. It would have been better for him to fall in the front of battle, where he had so often distinguished himself.

It was hard to give him up; yet all the probabilities were, that he had been killed, and that his body lay unnoticed and unhonored on the spot where he had fallen. Somers was a prisoner himself, and had been plundered even of the most necessary articles of wearing apparel, and subjected to needless insult and brutality The condition of the Union prisoners at Richmond, Andersonville, and Salisbury was too well known to him to render the prospect before him even tolerable. But a desponding spirit would only aggravate his miseries, and he determined to submit to his fate with patient resignation. He felt that he was in the keeping of the good Father, who doeth all things well; and in His appointed time he would be rescued from peril and restored to his friends; or, if it was the will of Heaven that he should lay down his life in grief and misery for the cause he had chosen to serve, he would try to be faithful and patient unto the bitter end.

The rebels conducted him through the woods to the creek, which they forded, and continued on their way till they reached a grove, where it now appeared that they had picketed their horses. It was also evident to the unfortunate prisoner that his captors were not regular cavalrymen, but guerillas, who hung on the flanks of the army to rob the wounded, plunder the dead, capture stragglers worth the trouble, and gather up the spoils of battle. When this was apparent to Somers, from the words and the actions of the wretches, he felt that he had reason to be thankful that they had not murdered him, as they probably had his friend. His life had been spared, but this new revelation of the character of his captors suggested a doubt whether death was not preferable to captivity in the hands of such miscreants. At the grove the men halted.

"Now, cap'n, off with them boots!" said Turkin, in savage tones.

Somers felt that he had not a moment's lease of life secured to him, and he promptly complied with the unreasonable demand of the guerilla.

"Who's gwine to hev them boots?" suggested one of the gang.

"The man as they fits," replied Turkin, who proceeded at once to try them on.

"No, sir! I'll be dog-on'd if anything of that sort shall be did!" protested the other.

"Well, Gragg, what's the use of them boots to you? You couldn't put 'em outside yer feet, more'n yer could crawl inter the barrel of yer shooter."

"May be I couldn't; but them boots is wuth more to you than the hoss. Draw lots fur 'em."

The guerillas debated this question for some time, and with so much acrimony that Somers ventured to hope they would resort to knives and bullets in the adjustment of the quarrel, and thus afford him an opportunity to profit by the discussion. But it was finally agreed to value the property, and make an equal division of it. Turkin could not get the boots on; whereat he was greatly enraged, and looked at Somers as though he intended to annihilate him for not having a larger foot. A young fellow of the party succeeded in getting them on, and they were apportioned to him. It was pleasant to think that he was dooming himself to a great deal of misery by his apparent good fortune; for, if he had corns, the boots would be agony to him; if not, they would be tight enough to raise a crop of the tormentors in a very brief period. If through tribulation we are brought to the truth, it is to be hoped that the sufferings of the young guerilla brought him to a belief that " honesty is the best policy," though this is not the highest rule of morality.

Each of the marauders was supplied with a horse, and apparently to save the trouble of leading him, rather than for the comfort of the prisoner, Somers was ordered to ride the animal which had belonged to De Banyan. The party were loaded with plunder, taken from the dead and wounded of both armies, as Somers judged from the appearance of the articles. They moved in the direction of the rebel camps, and in a short time they had passed beyond the reach of danger from the Union army.

" Gragg, what we gwine to do with this feller?" said Turkin, as he pointed to the prisoner. " We don't want him."

" Knock him on the head, and leave him here," replied the benevolent Gragg.

"I don't keer," added Turkin, as he rubbed his matted hair beneath his hat, as if to stimulate a half developed idea which was struggling for existence in his brain.

Somers did care: it would make considerable difference to him. He had patiently submitted to the policy of his captors in order to save his life; but upon the question of murdering him in cold blood, he felt that he had something to say. If resorting to desperate measures would afford the slightest hope of escape, he was ready to accept the issue. There were seven of the guerillas, and resistance was almost hopeless, yet not entirely so, for there was a single favorable circumstance to aid him.

As the prisoner rode along between Turkin and Gragg, he happened to discover that the holsters of De Banyan's horse still contained the pistols of his friend. They were two navy revolvers, which the guerillas had neglected to secure. With these formidable weapons Somers believed that he could make a tolerably good fight, though such a course would be madness on his part, unless he was reduced to the most desperate extremity, when death was certain if he did not resort to it.

"We don't want ter be bothered with this carri'n," continued the philanthropic Gragg.

"I was thinkin'," said Turkin.

"Was yer?" demanded Gragg, as the thinker did

not develop the result of his meditations. "What was yer thinkin'?"

"Yer know what happened yesterday?"

Gragg did know, and as it appeared from their conversation, Colonel Grayhame, of the Confederate cavalry, had threatened to hang the whole of the gang for some irregular proceedings among the rebel wounded.

"The kun'l's down on us, Gragg," added the politic Turkin.

"I don't keer."

"He'll spile our prospects. We kin make him good natered by givin' him a young scrub of a Yankee officer like this."

"I don't keer."

"It won't cost nothin'. We don't want the young cub; and he'll think we're doin' sunthin' for the cause."

"He'll make yer give up the boots and the coat," suggested the prudent Gragg.

"You bet he won't!" replied Turkin, positively. "The feller is a staff officer, belongin' to one of the big Yankee gin'rals; and the kun'l will be glad to git him."

"But the coat and the boots, the watch and the money? The kun'l's foolish about sech things. He don't take 'em from the Yanks."

It was finally decided to say that the prisoner had been robbed of these articles before they captured him, and to deliver the captive to the colonel, as a conciliatory offering. Somers was much relieved when this decision was reached, for it was some satisfaction to be handed over to an officer who was a gentleman, and had some regard for the comfort of his prisoners.

When the guerillas arrived at the spot where the camp of Colonel Grayhame had been on the previous day, their plans were entirely changed by learning that the cavalry under his command had been ordered away to look after the Union force, sent down to destroy the West Point Railroad; not that this information affected their purposes, but because it suggested a field for the better prosecution of their irregular work. Somers heard them discuss the matter; and he found that they believed the Union cavalry would burn and plunder public and private property, without discrimination, wherever they went. Their presence would create a panic; houses would be abandoned, citizens killed, and the spoils would be plentiful. When Turkin suggested that the party should follow the colonel, and gather up the plunder, his companions readily assented.

Somers did not learn what was to be done with himself, but he concluded that he was to go with them. Though it was now dark, the guerillas immediately started for the new field of operations, and the prisoner was placed between Gragg and Turkin, as before. These worthies were less communicative during the evening than they had been immediately after his capture, and Somers listened in vain for any hint in regard to the disposition which they intended to make of him.

They rode till about nine o'clock, when Gragg suggested that they were human, and ought to have some supper. They were approaching the mansion of a planter, and as they owed allegiance to neither side in the great conflict, it mattered but little to them who or what the owner was. Their sympathies were undoubtedly with the South, but their love of plunder was stronger than their sympathies.

"Git off the hoss, cap'n," said Turkin, as the party halted in the yard of the house.

Somers obeyed. In the darkness of the evening he had contrived to remove one of the revolvers from its holster, and place it under his vest; for he did not know that he should again be permitted to mount the horse. He had also transferred from a leather bag on the pommel of the saddle, two or three at a time, a sufficient number of patent cartridges and caps. He was not without a hope that the present halt would afford him an opportunity to attempt an escape.

"Lead your horse to the stable," added Turkin.

He put the horse in the stable with the others; but he was closely watched all the time. While he was thus engaged, he saw Gragg and Turkin in close conversation; and, though Somers could not hear what was said, he was satisfied that they were talking about him.

"Cap'n," said Turkin, as the prisoner came out of the stall.

"I am here," replied Somers.

"Will you be shot afore supper, or arter?"

"Neither."

"That's jest what I expected you mought say, because it stands to reason no man don't want to be shot."

"Just my sentiments; I don't want to be shot."

"Jes so; and yer ought to be much obleeged ter me fur not shoot'n yer before."

"I am very grateful to you for your consideration."

"Exac'ly; you ain't no more use to us than a knife and fork to a cow."

"I don't do you any harm."

"That may be; but yer don't do no good. Cap'n, will yer be shot afore supper, or arter?" repeated Turkin.

"I have already expressed my views on that subject."

"Yes or no?"

"No."

"Cap'n, you kin read, I take it."

"I can."

"D'yer ever read the story about the monkey that took the cat's paw to haul the chestnuts out the fire with?"

"I have."

"I knew yer hed; yer Yanks is great readers. Do yer know what the moril is to that story?"

"I think I do."

"I knew yer did; yer Yanks is great on morils. I'm gwine ter tell yer the moril of that story. Did yer say you'd be shot afore supper, or arter?"

"Neither, if it will accommodate you just as well," replied Somers, greatly perplexed to know what the fellow was going to do.

"Never mind, then; we'll talk about the moril. It ain't jest the thing fur us to go inter this house, and make 'em get supper fur us, because we ain't exac'ly reg'lar. We wan't the supper, and we may want sunthin' more, arter that. We don't want to be seen in the business. Now, we are the monkey, and you are the cat's paw — don't yer see?"

"I don't quite understand you."

"You shall go in, order the supper, and do the talkin' for us. When they git supper ready, we'll go in and eat it, without any of the folks seein' on us. Yer'll be cap'n, and do the talkin' for us — don't yer see?"

"I see."

"And keep the folks from seein' us too — don't yer see?"

"I see."

"Now, cap'n, will yer be shot afore supper, or arter?" demanded Turkin.

"Neither," replied Somers, thereby consenting to the plan proposed by the guerilla.

## CHAPTER XXVI.

### SUPPER FOR SEVEN.

WHATEVER the merits of the plan in which Somers was compelled to take a part, he did not relish the idea of being made a cat's paw in the hands of such unmitigated villains as the guerillas. It involved no sacrifice of principle, and did not require him to give "aid and comfort to the enemy;" otherwise he would have taken his chances in an encounter with the whole squad. It was one portion of the enemy feeding on another portion; and if the planter, who was himself a rebel, objected to the forced contribution, he had only to thank himself for the state of things he had assisted in bringing about.

"I am ready," said Somers, when Turkin had fully explained his plan.

"We're all half starved, and I cal'late we're ready too."

"But do you think I shall look much like an officer, when I go in without any coat or boots?"

"May be we mought lend you a coat," replied Turkin, struck with the force of the suggestion.

By his order, Somers's coat was restored to him, with the remark that he would not want it after supper; which led him to believe that he was to be shot when the wretches had no further use for him.

"An officer usually wears a sword," added Somers, "and a pair of boots."

"Ger 'long!" said Gragg.

"Do you think an officer would be without boots, when all his men are so well shod? I think I should be a cat's paw without any claws."

"Give him his boots; he won't want 'em arter supper," replied Turkin; and the young man who had these useful articles was compelled to pull them off, which he did with a great deal of difficulty.

Somers put them on, and began to feel like himself again.

"See here, cap'n; couldn't you send the folks all out the house for a while, when we are at supper?"

"Perhaps I could; but I fancy they will think I am a humbug, when I go in without a sword."

"Give him his sword," said Turkin. "Now, kin yer send the folks off?—play 'em some Yankee trick? —don't yer see?"

"Perhaps I could; I'll try."

"Ef yer do well, we'll give yer supper afore—"

"You git!" said Gragg, expressively.

"I'll do the best I can," replied Somers, confirmed in

his opinion that the savages meant to kill him, by the interrupted remark of Turkin, and the expressive tones of Gragg.

"Kin yer write, Yank?" asked Turkin.

"I can."

"I knew yer could; yer Yanks is great at writin'. Write 'em a note, sayin' somebody wants ter see 'em down to the next house."

"Capital!" exclaimed Somers. "I should think you were a Yankee yourself."

"Don't call me a Yank."

"I only meant that you can beat the Yankees at playing tricks."

"I'm some."

All the servants outside the house had been captured, and kept in the darkness, where they could not recognize any of the guerillas. They had already been questioned, and enough was known of the family to enable Somers to write a note; but they had no paper.

"I can manage it," said Somers, suddenly, as though a splendid suggestion had occurred to him. "If I take from my Testament one of those pictures, and tell them the person represented wishes to see them, they will go. If they don't recognize the picture, they will be the more curious to know who it is."

"May be they will," replied Turkin, doubtfully.

But it appeared from the story of the negroes that a son

of the gentleman in the next house had married a daughter of the planter; that both were at Savannah; and it was finally agreed that the spokesman of the party should say the daughter had suddenly arrived, was quite ill, and wished all the family would come down and see her.

"But I want one of those pictures to write the message on," added Somers.

"I'll give yer one."

"And I want to take it from the Testament. It will look more natural."

The guerillas thought so too, and by the light of the lantern which one of the negroes brought, he wrote in pencil, "*These villains mean to rob your house after supper; get a force and capture them.*"

"He's great at writin'— ain't he?" said the admiring Turkin.

"Will you look at it?" asked Somers, innocently.

Turkin took the card, and looked at it steadily by the light of the lantern for a moment, and then handed it back to the writer.

"That will do, you bet," added Turkin. "We're great on a trick — ain't we?"

"There's nothing like a well-managed trick," answered Somers, as he placed the card in the Testament, which had been given him for the purpose. "You are sharp fellows, and this thing will work to a charm."

"I cal'late it will; but ger 'long; we want our supper. After that we'll show you a trick wuth two of that."

They walked to the side door of the house, which was some distance from the stable, so that the arrival of the guerillas had not been noticed by the people within. The villains seemed to have a very wholesome dread of Colonel Grayhame, for they often alluded to him in connection with the present operation; and they had already discovered that his main force was not far in advance of them, while detachments of his regiment were guarding the railroad, not half a mile from the house.

"See here, Yank; I don't know as we kin trust yer," said Turkin, who had accompanied him to the door, leaving his companions in an arbor, within hail of the mansion.

"I don't care whether you do or not," answered Somers. "This isn't my job; it is yours."

"I'll go in with yer, with my face kivered up, and if yer don't talk right up, I shan't ask yer whether yer'll be shot afore supper or arter."

"I'll do just what you tell me to do."

"Ger 'long, then."

Somers knocked at the door, which seemed to displease his rude companion, who wished him to walk in without any ceremony; but the "cat's paw" explained that a certain degree of courtesy would help the enterprise, and the guerilla assented, though with an ill grace. The door was opened by a sleek, black servant.

"Is Colonel Roman within?" asked Somers, using the name of the planter which had been given him by Turkin.

"Yes, sar."

"I wish to see him."

"Walk in, sar."

Somers was conducted to an elegant library, where the planter and his family were seated. He was closely followed by Turkin, who had tied a red silk handkerchief over his face, so that his ugly physiognomy was entirely concealed from the inmates of the room. The planter rose from his chair, and bowed with stately courtesy to his unexpected visitors.

"I beg your pardon for disturbing you, Colonel Roman," said Somers.

"Whom have I the honor of addressing?" demanded the planter, rather coldly.

"Captain Somers, of the army, at your service, sir."

"You seem to wear the uniform of the Yankees."

"That's inter yer," whispered Turkin, who stood close by his spokesman.

"I was so fortunate as to obtain this uniform from a Yankee officer whom I captured," replied Somers, with promptness.

"There yer hev him," added Turkin.

"That explains it, though some officers prefer to go in rags rather than wear the colors of the Yankees, especially when obtained in that manner."

"I have only to say, sir, that the Yankee from whom I got them had no further use for his clothes," added Somers, pleased to find that the chivalry did not justify the system which prevailed of robbing prisoners of their clothing.

"May I ask your business with me, sir?"

"I have a small squad of seven men with me. We have had no supper, and we wish to trespass so far on your hospitality as to obtain one in your house."

"Eight of you?" asked the planter. "You shall be supplied at once."

"We are in great haste."

"All possible expedition shall be used in preparing the meal," answered the planter, as he ordered his servant to give the proper directions to the cook and others. "Do you belong to Colonel Grayhame's force?"

"Tell him yer do," whispered Turkin.

"We do, sir. We stopped at the next house below, to get some supper, for we are almost starved; but they had just received some friends from Savannah, and could not provide for us."

"From Savannah?" said the planter, with evident surprise; and immediately the ladies present suspended their sewing, and looked at the young officer.

"Yer smart, Yank!" muttered Turkin, who appeared to enjoy the situation amazingly.

"I think they said from Savannah," replied Somers

"They recommended us to come here, assuring us that you never turned a hungry soldier from your door. They gave me a card, requesting me to deliver it to you."

Somers handed the planter the photograph, on the back of which was written the appalling statement of the character of the guerillas. It was a fearful moment to him, for the alarm of the planter might betray him to the bloodthirsty villain who stood at his side. Though the silk handkerchief over the face of Turkin impaired his vision, it did not entirely obstruct it.

Colonel Roman read the words on the card; he was startled by them, and glanced at the bearer of the message. Somers contracted his brow, shook his head slightly in the direction of Turkin, and assumed a deprecatory expression, which the planter seemed to understand.

"The persons at the next house wish to see you as soon as possible," added Somers.

"We will go at once," replied Colonel Roman, "if you will excuse my absence."

"Certainly, sir," answered Somers, now fully assured that he was understood.

"What is it, father?" asked one of the daughters, puzzled by the remarks which had been made in her presence.

"Your sister Lucretia has arrived from Savannah;

she is ill, and we will go down and see her immediately," replied the planter.

The wife and both of the daughters expressed their surprise; but the colonel directed them to get ready as speedily as possible, and they left the room for this purpose.

"I am sorry to leave you, captain," continued the planter; "but I will endeavor to return as soon as you have finished your supper. Pray make yourselves entirely at home. Why don't your men come into the house. My doors are always open to the defenders of my country."

"Thank you, Colonel Roman. I will take them into the dining-room at once."

"Do so," said the planter, as he left the room.

"You're smart, Yank!" exclaimed Turkin.

"I have only done what you told me to do. If there is any credit about the affair, it belongs to you," replied Somers, in a deprecatory tone.

"That's so, Yank; but yer kerried it through right smart, and yer shall hev some supper afore —"

"You are shot," the ruffian would have said, if not prevented by prudential motives.

The planter and his family left the house by the front door; and it is probable that they used all possible haste to escape from the presence of the guerillas, whose character they now understood. In the mean time, Turkin amused himself by opening the various drawers in the planter's secretary, and prying into every hole and corner which might be supposed to contain any valuables.

In half an hour, supper was announced, and Turkin went to the dining-room. The servants were sent off, and ordered not to show themselves again. The guerillas then sat down to supper, making Somers stand before the door leading into the hall, to notify them of the approach of any person. They ate and drank, but they did not hear the sounds of horses' hoofs in the yard, just as they finished their meal.

## CHAPTER XXVII.

#### THE CAT'S PAW TOO SHARP FOR THE MONKEY.

THE side door of the house opened into the hall, where Somers stood as sentinel for the hungry guerillas, and from which a flight of stairs led to the second floor. The prisoner had carefully noted all the surroundings, for he had learned from "Fighting Joe" that the battle was gained only by good strategy, which must depend upon a thorough knowledge of the ground.

When the precious plan of his captors was first developed, Somers regarded it as the means of his deliverance, though he could not then tell precisely in what manner it was to be accomplished. He knew that an important bridge on the railroad, not far from Colonel Roman's house, was guarded by a squad of cavalry, and he readily perceived that this force would be brought up by the planter for the protection of his family and the capture of the guerillas. These wretches were by no means an anomalous class on the flanks of Sherman's grand march to the sea; and Colonel Roman readily understood who and what they were. They were nominally southern partisans, organized, protected, and encouraged by the president of the Confederate States; but they were as willing to plunder one party in the strife as the other.

Somers had no special sympathy for the planter, though he would have gladly raised his arm in defence of the female members of his family, even against the wretches whom treason and rebellion had brought into the field. What he had done was for his own benefit, rather than for that of the hospitable rebel. He had recovered possession of his boots and coat, his Testament and photographs, when he became the "cat's paw" of the guerillas, and he was now in condition to make a movement as soon as the circumstances would justify it.

The land-pirates — for they can be called by no more appropriate name — finished their supper, and turned their attention to the second part of the programme they had laid out. Evidently they did not intend to sack the mansion, but only to appropriate such valuable small articles as could be conveniently carried about their persons. For this purpose Turkin and Gragg entered the library; two others crossed the hall into the sitting-room; and the other three went up stairs. They had not heard the tramp of horses in the yard; but Somers, being near the side door, which was partly open, listened to the sounds as the notes of his own deliverance.

The time for action had come, and while the guerillas were intent upon their plunder, Somers left the door where he had been stationed, and moved round to the rear of the staircase, where he expected to find a passage to the cellar; but he found none. The house was surrounded by rebel cavalry, and it was not safe for him to go out, for he did not forget that it was necessary for him to escape from the foe without, as well as the foe within. They were both enemies; and though one was less barbarous than the other, he had hardly more relish for Andersonville, than for being shot by the wretches who held him.

As the only alternative, he went up the stairs; and avoiding the three men who were searching the chambers there, he found the garret steps, and went up, where he was not likely to be followed by any of his late companions. He had scarcely reached this secure position before the commotion below indicated that the cavalrymen had commenced their work. One or two shots were fired; but the noise immediately subsided, and it was evident that the robbers had all been captured.

"There were eight of them, you said," Somers heard some one in the entry below remark.

"There were; but one of them was the officer who gave the information," replied another, whom the fugitive recognized as Colonel Roman.

"But he was one of the gang."

"He looked like a Yankee officer," added the colonel.

"We want him, whatever he is, if it is only for his evidence against these villains we have captured. Colonel Grayhame threatened to hang these same scoundrels only yesterday."

"The officer who gave me the card is clearly not one of this gang."

"I don't understand it," said the other person, who was probably the officer in command of the squad of cavalry.

"I should be very glad of an explanation, but I am greatly indebted to the gentleman, and I wish to thank him, if nothing more, for the favor he has done me," continued the colonel.

"I have nothing against him, but I wish to know what he is."

Somers hoped he would not trouble himself, and he was even willing the planter should omit to thank him; for the officer's curiosity and the colonel's gratitude threatened to consign him to a rebel prison. He heard a call from the former, followed by the tramp of heavy feet on the lower staircase.

"Lieutenant, I hope you will consider my position in this matter," said the planter.

"I must do my duty. If the man is a Yankee officer, as you think, he must not be permitted to roam around the country. He may belong to the force which is now destroying the railroad; perhaps gobbled up by these miscreants. It is not for me to say what shall be done with him. I must catch him if I can. I saw him standing at the door of the dining-room, when I looked in at the window, and I am positive he has not left the house."

"I regard the person as my friend," added the planter, warmly. "My wife and daughters, as well as myself, are very grateful to him, for he has saved them from insult and outrage, for aught I know."

"Your feelings and those of your family shall be respected, Colonel Roman; but I must do my duty," answered the lieutenant, firmly.

The officer then ordered his men to search the various apartments and closets of the second floor. Somers, though the case certainly looked very hopeful for him, with the powerful influence of the wealthy planter in his favor, wished to escape; but he thought it would be an easy and safe thing to return to Sherman's army before Atlanta, and he was not disposed to be introduced to the lieutenant, or even to improve his acquaintance with Colonel Roman. If he could conceal himself until the squad of cavalry retired, he was satisfied that the planter would enable him to return to the army.

It was very dark in the garret, and while the lieutenant and his party were searching the chambers, Somers carefully felt about him for some place of concealment. The roof was a four-sided one, in which there were no windows; but while he was walking about, he struck his head against a long iron handle, which proved to be attached to a shutter or scuttle. This he unfastened and raised, and his eyes were greeted by a view of the starry sky. The discovery was a welcome one, and he lost not a moment in availing himself of the advantage which it seemed to afford.

The lower end of the aperture was within reach of his hands; and with great care and no little difficulty he raised himself, and succeeded in gaining the roof — an operation which his gymnastic practice enabled him to accomplish, for it was a feat an untrained person could hardly have performed. But he had scarcely reached the roof before he heard his pursuers in the attic, and the light from their lamps shone up through the scuttle.

"I see where he has gone!" shouted the lieutenant, as he discovered the open shutter.

"He will fall and break his neck," added the planter.

Somers closed the scuttle, and sat down upon it; but the game seemed to be up with him. He drew his sword, and thrust the point into the roof as far as he could, causing it to act as a bolt over the shutter — hoping by this means to gain a moment's time to examine the situation. There appeared to be no means of descending from the roof to the ground except by the lightning-rods, which he saw rising above the chimneys. Then, if he reached the ground, the house was surrounded by rebels, and his fate would only be deferred.

While he was considering these facts, the men in the attic were endeavoring to raise the scuttle. They did not at once succeed; but Somers's prospects were presently destroyed, when several of the rebels took hold of the shutter and raised it, tumbling the fugitive over on the roof. A short ladder was placed on the floor, and the lieutenant mounted to the top of the house.

"Surrender!" said the officer.

"I suppose there is no help for it," replied Somers.

"Not the least; resistance would be useless."

"I surrender."

"Go down, then, if you please."

Somers descended the ladder to the garret, where he found Colonel Roman and half a dozen cavalrymen.

"I am sorry you are taken, since you did not wish to be taken," said the planter.

"I could not very well help myself."

The lieutenant led the way down stairs to the library, which was the largest room in the house, and in which the seven guerillas, now disarmed, were held by their captors.

"Well, Yank, you be counted in with us," said Turkin, with a malicious grin.

"I have the satisfaction of escaping from your hands, if nothing more," replied Somers.

"See here, Yank; I cal'lated to shoot you after supper, but I reckon we'll all hang together."

"I think not," interposed the lieutenant; "you have said enough already to convince me that this gentleman does not belong to your gang."

"He's a Yank; we took him over yender, and he belongs to some gin'ral's staff. I reckon he's a good haul, and I ought to hev the credit of ketchin' him."

"Your accounts will be settled in a few days; and I fancy Colonel Grayhame will hang you higher than Haman, when he understands this business."

"That would be moighty onhandsome, arter we ketched the Yankee officer."

"Your name, if you please, sir," said the lieutenant, turning to the prisoner.

"Captain Thomas Somers," replied he, at the same time giving his official position and connections.

"You were captured by these men?"

"I was;" and Somers detailed the particulars of the event. "Major de Banyan was shot at the same time," he added, turning to Turkin, who, he hoped, would endeavor to improve his prospects by telling what had become of his friend.

"I shot him," said Gragg; "and if I'm to be hung fur that, I cal'late it won't be safe to fight the Yanks much longer."

"Was he killed?" asked the lieutenant.

"I reckon he wan't; we got him over the creek; there he gin out, and we left him, and stivered back arter his hoss. That's when we took this Yank; but Turkin shot his hoss instid of him."

" Was the major dead when you left him?"

" Not jest then; but I cal'late he didn't stand it long."

Somers's worst fears in regard to his friend seemed to be confirmed. To the questions of the officer he gave true answers, until the history of the guerillas' movements up to the time of their arrival at the mansion of the planter had been elicited.

" I was made the cat's paw of these men, who wished to procure a supper, and to rob the house without exposing themselves to detection. Their purpose was to get the family out of the house," continued Somers. " You did not find your friends from Savannah at the next house — did you, Colonel Roman?"

" I did not expect to find them there. Was that your scheme?"

" You bet it wan't, kun'l," exclaimed Turkin, as though he feared Somers would obtain more credit than he deserved. " That's some of my thinkin', kun'l. The Yank ain't so good on tricks as I be. I told him what to write on that keerd. The Yank is great at writin', but I'm some for plannin'."

" Did you read what he wrote on the card?" asked Colonel Roman, who could not help laughing at the simplicity of the wretch.

" I reckon I didn't; I ain't much at readin' writin'."

"I will read it to you," added the planter, taking the card from his pocket: "'*These villains mean to rob your house after supper; get a force and capture them.*'"

"Is that what he writ?" demanded Turkin, in a fearful rage.

"It is. The cat's paw had a fang."

"Then I'll hang him."

"You will be hung yourself first."

Everything was explained; and now came up the question in regard to the disposition of Somers. The lieutenant declared he had no authority to discharge the prisoner, who was a Union officer; but he would report the case to his superiors.

"That's inter yer, Yank," said Turkin. "You'll go with us."

Colonel Roman interposed to prevent Somers's longer remaining in the company of the villains. The prisoner gave his parole for three days, and the officer left him with the planter, who promised to go with him to the headquarters of the rebel army within that time. The lieutenant then departed with his prisoners, and Somers was treated as a guest in the house of the colonel.

## CHAPTER XXVIII.

#### THE BLOOD-HOUNDS ON THE TRACK.

IN one week from the day on which Somers made the acquaintance of Colonel Roman, he was inside of the stockade at Andersonville. It so happened that the general officer with whom rested the decision in the case of the prisoner, was a personal and political opponent of the planter, and the colonel had no influence with him. An appeal was made to higher authority, but it was unavailing; and Somers was hurried away to that miserable place, where officers and soldiers died by thousands, of sheer inhumanity.

Colonel Roman promised to continue his exertions for the release of his friend, or, if he could not obtain that, for better treatment than had usually been accorded to prisoners of war by the Confederacy. It is quite probable that he did so, but the subject of his intercession obtained no favor on account of it. His experience at Andersonville was that of thousands of others. It would require a volume to narrate it; and the sad story has been so often told, that it needs not a repetition here. The whole civilized world condemns the barbarous treatment of prisoners by the Confederacy.

Week after week, and month after month, dragged away amid suffering and privation, until Sherman's grand march to the sea filled the rebels with terror; and a portion of the prisoners remaining in their hands were sent to Columbia, South Carolina. Somers was among the number. He had been a prisoner for nearly five months, and his health was already much impaired by his sufferings; by the scanty and mean food, but quite as much by being compelled to witness the misery and death which prevailed in the horrid slaughter-pen in which he had been confined. Once he had made an attempt to escape, but had been hunted down and recaptured.

He arrived at Columbia; but he had made up his mind not to stay there. It was sure death to one of his temperament to live such a dog's life as that to which he had been doomed. It was better to be shot down by the sentinels, or even to be torn in pieces by the fangs of the merciless blood-hounds, than to die by inches within the camp of the prisoners.

Every day a certain number of prisoners, paroled for the purpose, were allowed to go out after wood, for two hours. Those who were thus favored were obliged to sign a parole, and their names were handed to the officer of the day, who was authorized to permit them to pass. When Somers found an opportunity to join one of these parties, he gave his parole, as others did; and even his sufferings had not so far demoralized him that he could violate the solemn pledge. He went out with the others, but immediately returned with his load of wood. Hastening to the officer of the day, he told him he had done his share of the work, and requested to be released from his parole, which was then given back to him. He was now free from his obligation, and having destroyed the paper, if he should happen to be recaptured in his attempt to escape, it could not be brought against him to subject him to the penalty of its violation.

Others were bringing in wood and timber, and passing out again for more. Somers walked out with the rest. When they came to the guard they were carefully examined again, to see that none but paroled officers passed out. They gave their names, and the sentinel referred to the list of those paroled for that day, and if it was all right, they were allowed to pass.

"Your name?" said the guard to Somers.

The prisoner gave it.

"All right," replied the sentinel, who, of course, found the name in the list.

Somers was now outside of the camp, and discharged from his parole; but his difficulties had only just commenced, for a guard of eighty men was stretched around the tract of woods in which the prisoners were at work. He walked away from the stockade animated by a hope, though it was but a dim one, of breathing once more the air of freedom. Intent upon the object before him, he passed a group of emaciated forms, whose constitutions were strong enough to enable them to overcome the horrors of the hospital, in which they were still patients.

"Somers!" exclaimed one of them, rushing towards him.

The young officer turned, and in the tall, pale, attenuated person who addressed him, he recognized his friend De Banyan. He looked like a wreck, and there was little to remind him of the manly and noble form of the major, as he had known him five months before.

"De Banyan!" cried Somers, rushing into the arms of his friend, and weeping like a child with the joy he could not conceal.

It was a tender and a touching reunion, and even the rebel sentinels did not interpose to separate them.

"How came you here?" demanded De Banyan, when the first emotions of the happy meeting had subsided.

"I was captured at the time you were shot; but I have been at Andersonville till a week ago," replied Somers.

"I have been in the hospital; that's the reason I did not see you."

"That must be the reason," replied Somers, in a loud tone; and then, dropping his voice to a whisper, he added, "I am going to escape to-day."

"I have been quite sick," continued the major, aloud. "I am on parole" — in a whisper.

"Are you better?"

"Much better; I feel pretty well now," said the major. "Wait half an hour for me in the woods."

"I will," replied Somers, as he moved on.

De Banyan soon joined him. At his own request the surgeon had discharged him, and he had taken up his parole. With a basket of vials, which he found in an ante-room of the hospital, he walked boldly through the guards, who, believing him still to be a paroled prisoner, permitted him to pass. During his convalescence, he had been employed in various light duties connected with the hospital, and had had frequent occasion to pass the sentries, so that no suspicion attached to him after he had been relieved from his parole.

With Somers he walked to the woods, and with him chopped and gathered sticks. At a point near the centre of the space surrounded by the sentinels, they found a pine tree, whose dense foliage promised to afford them the shelter they required. At a favorable moment Somers sprang up into the tree, and the major followed him a few minutes later. Of course they were seen by their fellow-prisoners, and they were obliged to run the risk of being exposed by any one of them who was vile enough to do such a mean act. Men have been known at Andersonville, Columbia, and other prison camps, to stoop to the contemptible and cowardly meanness of betraying a comrade under such circumstances; but with only a few rare exceptions, the prisoners were too manly and noble to be guilty of such a base act.

They had escaped the observation of the soldiers, who were too indolent, or too far off, to notice what took place within their line. The only duty they were called upon to perform, as they seemed to regard it, was to prevent any of the prisoners from passing beyond the bounds allotted to them. The two hours in which the men were allowed to gather wood expired soon after Somers and De Banyan ascended the tree.

"Good by, Captain; report me at home, if you get through," said a Massachusetts officer, who stood at the foot of the tree when the prisoners were ordered back to the camp.

"I will," replied Somers, who knew the officer's address.

The prisoners, laden with their sticks of timber and bundles of wood, were driven back to the camp, to endure other weeks and months of suffering, or to die there, as many had done before. Somers and the major kept perfectly still until the guard had passed the tree, and disappeared from their view.

"We shall be missed before long," said Somers.

"We will not stop here," replied De Banyan, as he descended the tree and lay down on the ground at the foot of it.

Somers followed him, lying down by his side. Having satisfied themselves that they had not been observed, they crawled away until the slope of a hill concealed them from the view of the camp, when they ventured to stand upright, like men, and press forward for life and liberty. They continued to walk in a southerly direction till they came to a creek, over which they swam, in the hope that the water would interrupt the scent of the blood-hounds which would be put on their track as soon as their absence was discovered.

It was a vain hope. They were in a kind of swampy jungle, not more than half a mile from the creek, when they heard the fearful cry of the dogs.

"We are lost!" exclaimed Somers, appalled at the horrible sounds.

"No!" replied De Banyan, with his old energy. "Don't give it up!"

"I won't, if you do not," added Somers, inspired with courage by the firmness and self-possession of his friend.

"Find a club, if you can!"

They were fortunate enough to find a couple of sticks, soaked full of water, with which they hoped to make a good fight.

"Shall we climb a tree?" asked Somers.

"You are lost if you do," replied De Banyan, as he took from his pocket a roll of cord, which he had appropriated in the hospital for another purpose.

Unrolling it, he cut it into two pieces, with one of which he made a slip-noose, and directed Somers to do the same with the other. The dogs were still some distance from the spot, and the men in pursuit seemed to be unable to follow them on their horses, which explained the major's policy in choosing a swamp for his flight. Selecting a narrow pass between two clumps of bushes, which had been beaten into a path, he stretched the slip-noose over it, just as boys in the country set snares for foxes and rabbits. Somers did precisely the same thing in another locality.

De Banyan then bent down a small sapling, so that the top of it came over the snare, and attached the end of the cord to it. The little tree was held down by weaving the branches into the bushes, just strong enough to hold it down, but so that any force beyond its own elasticity would disengage it. The contrivance formed what is sometimes called a "twitch-up snare." Somers knew all about it, and set his own in the same manner.

By this time the dogs were upon them, and each of them stepped behind the trap he had set. The hounds made directly towards them, two by one path and one by the other.

"Come on, doggy," said De Banyan, as he stood coolly waiting the issue of the enterprise. "Stand by with your club, Somers, if it fails."

"I am all ready," replied Somers, as he nerved his arm for the conflict, if one should be necessary.

On rushed the blood-hounds, with their fiendish yelp, the one that approached De Banyan being a few feet in advance of the others. He dashed into the narrow path, thrusting his head through the noose, drawing it tight around his neck, and detaching the tree. The elasticity of the sapling gave him a tremendous twitch, and lifted his fore legs from the ground. The spring was not strong enough to hold his whole weight, and the hound hung by the neck, partially supported by his hind legs.

Somers's snare was not quite so successful; but the spring choked the dog, and held him fast. The third hound, dodging the obstruction in his path, rushed towards him from another direction; but De Banyan was at his side by this time, and with a few heavy blows, they killed the ugly beast. Of the other two, one was nearly choked to death, but both were quickly despatched with the clubs.

"That job is done," said De Banyan.

"And well done," replied Somers, as they resumed their flight.

## CHAPTER XXIX.

### THE PILGRIMAGE TO THE SEA.

IT was not very easy travelling in the swamp, but it had this advantage, that they could not be pursued by cavalry. They had silenced the howl of the dogs, and their pursuers could have no idea of the direction they had taken. The killing of the blood-hounds gave the fugitives all the advantage, and they "doubled" on the hunters by returning to the creek which they had crossed before. After following the stream for about five miles, as there were no signs of a pursuit in this direction, they halted to wait for the protecting shades of night, when they hoped to find some of the negroes, whom recaptured prisoners had uniformly represented as kind and devoted to the last degree.

It would be several hours before the journey could be safely resumed, and our reunited friends had much to say of the past and the future. Each wished to know the history of the other since they had parted. Somers accounted for himself first, and De Banyan then exhibited the scar of an ugly wound in the head, which was the one given him by the guerilla. It had knocked him from his horse; but he had soon recovered his senses, and the villains had conducted him over the creek where he fainted. When he came to himself, his captors had left him; but he was soon picked up by a squad of the regular rebel cavalry, and sent first to the hospital, then to Columbia, where he had been from that time. He had fully recovered from his wound, but his health was much impaired by hard usage and poor food. He had gone to the hospital to die, as he thought; but his vigorous constitution enabled him to survive the medical treatment.

He had been too feeble to attempt to escape, as hundreds of others had done; but he was now in better condition than he had been before since his capture. In the hospital, by the exercise of his ingenuity, he had obtained better food, which had, in a measure, improved his health. The sight of Somers had given him new life and hope; and though he was but a shadow of his former self, he felt able to undergo all perils and privations on the road to liberty.

"I think we have avoided our pursuers," said Somers, when the major had finished his narrative. "What shall we do next?"

"Keep clear of the rebels, if we can; if we can't, bluff them off," replied De Banyan, hopefully.

"But where shall we go?"

"We must take the best route to the sea; perhaps the nearest is not the best. A great many men have escaped from Camp Sorghum, but I believe one half of them have been caught again."

"Then our chances are not first rate."

"They are very good, if we manage well. So far as I know, all who have had the escape fever attempt to reach the sea by the Santee River; and I fancy that river is pretty closely watched now."

"Then it is not best to go that way."

"No: about twenty miles from us to the southward, the road to Augusta crosses the Edisto River. I am in favor of taking that route, because I don't know that any of the prisoners have gone that way."

The point was settled, and as soon as it was dark, the fugitives started on their journey to the sea. Before night they had decided upon the direction of the Augusta road, and succeeded in reaching it. Both of them were in rags, and they were wet and cold. They had eaten nothing since morning, and the greatest obstacle with which they had now to contend was their own feebleness. They reached the road; but though the night was not half gone, they were completely exhausted. They were too cold to sit down and rest, and the exercise of walking seemed to impart no warmth to their weak and almost bloodless frames. They were not in condition to encounter the hardships in their path.

De Banyan, with his soul of iron, gave out first, and actually sank down by the side of the road. Somers could hardly keep from weeping when he realized the condition of his companion. He was not much stronger himself, and the enterprise promised to be an utter failure. It was the month of December; the air was chilly, and the ground cold and wet, and something must be done for the major, or he would perish before morning.

Somers was weak in body, but he was still strong in spirit. The condition of his friend appealed to him with an eloquence which he could not resist, and moved him to greater energy. Taking from the fence a number of rails, he made a kind of platform of them in a concealed spot in the field, which he covered with leaves, twigs, and cornstalks, obtained from an adjacent lot, until he had made a tolerably dry and comfortable bed. He conducted the major to his new quarters, and laid him on the couch he had prepared.

"Somers," said De Banyan, feebly.

"What shall I do for you now?"

"Nothing more, Somers. I am used up."

"You will be better soon."

"Never, my dear fellow."

"Don't give up."

"I wouldn't give up while there is a fibre left of me to lean on; but I am almost gone. Somers, take care of yourself now. You can do me no good; follow this road till you come to the river, and then find a boat, and float down to the blockading ships."

"I shall not leave you, De Banyan," exclaimed Somers, horrified by the suggestion.

"You can't do a thing for me. I shall die in a few hours. I didn't think I was so near gone when I left the camp, or I wouldn't have burdened you with the care of me."

"I should have been caught before this time, if it hadn't been for you. I will never desert you, De Banyan. God would not suffer me to live, if I should do so mean a thing!" replied Somers, earnestly.

"As you love me, Somers, save yourself. It would be the greatest favor you could do me to insure your own safety," replied the sufferer, in quivering tones.

"I will not leave you, but I will save you. I can and will," added Somers, with energy. "You shall not die. Keep a good heart for a little while, and you shall be saved."

"I will keep up as well as I can; but when a strong man, like me, sinks, he generally goes all at once. Leave me, I beg of you, Somers. It is the last favor I have to ask of you."

"I would not if you begged it on your bended knee. I must leave you for a time, but you shall be saved, if God will permit."

"God bless you, Somers," faintly ejaculated the sufferer.

Somers left him, and hastened back to the road, carefully noticing the path, so that he could easily find the spot again. When he reached it, he was almost overcome by his emotions, and by his own exhaustion. He wanted strength, at that trying moment, more than ever before in his life — strength to save himself and his friend. He knelt down upon the cold ground, and prayed for strength with an earnestness which had never before burned in his soul. He trusted in God, and he asked for guidance in this most trying experience of his life.

He rose from his knees. He knew that the good Father had heard him — was with him. Strength came, if not to his muscles, in the increased earnestness of his purpose. He walked along the road till he came to the house, which the cornfields he had seen assured him could not be far distant. It was the mansion of a large plantation, and beyond it was its village of negro huts. The blacks were friendly, but he could hardly expect to find among them what he required to restore the waning life of De Banyan.

Somers was a desperate man. It seemed to him then that the rebels had no rights which he was bound to respect. Throwing off his dilapidated boots, he approached the house, and went to one of the windows.

To his surprise he found it partly open. With all necessary care he raised the sash, and got into the house. There was just light enough in the room to enable him to find his way to the mantel, on which were a lamp and matches. He lighted the lamp and looked about him. There was a bed in the room, on which lay an object which would have frozen the blood in the veins of a timid person.

It was a corpse, the eyes covered with cents, enclosed in paper, and the jaw tied up with a handkerchief. Somers glanced at it: he was startled, but not appalled; for death, in its most horrid forms, was so familiar to him that he did not shrink from the sight. He had a mission to perform, and he proceeded to search the room for what he wanted. In a large closet he found two full suits of men's clothing, one of them a rebel uniform; and he concluded that the deceased had been an officer in the army. On a table, with a number of vials, he found a bottle of brandy, of which he drank a few swallows himself.

Dropping the clothing out of the window, where he could take it at his leisure, he continued the search, and found a couple of revolvers in a drawer, with caps and cartridges, which he appropriated. He then left the room, and in the hall found an overcoat; but the most needed articles were bacon and bread, of which he discovered a plentiful supply in another room. Filling a basket with the food, he hastened to make his escape.

"Is that you, Alfred?" said the voice of a woman on the second floor.

"Yes," replied Somers.

"Is everything right?"

"Yes."

"Don't you think you had better shut the windows? I am afraid some creature will get into the room."

"I will," answered Somers, afraid to use many words.

He crept back into the chamber of death, and respecting the fears of the woman, who might be the wife or the mother of the deceased, he closed three of the four windows, and when he had passed out himself, shut the remaining one. With the utmost care, he departed from the house laden with the precious articles he had obtained. It was one o'clock at night, as he had seen by a clock in the house, and all was still. At a safe distance from the mansion, he took off the rags he wore, and put on the rebel uniform, leaving the other suit, which was heavier and warmer, for De Banyan. Thus relieved of a portion of his burden, he hastened to the couch of his perishing companion.

"How do you feel, my best friend?" said Somers, as he bent over the sick man.

"Is that you, Somers? I hoped you had gone," replied the major, very faintly.

"No: I am come with life and hope," added Somers, as he placed the bottle of brandy to the sick man's lips.

He drank all that his faithful companion dared to give him. It warmed his stomach, and gave him new life.

"God bless you, Somers! I was thinking that brandy would save my life. I felt as though my vitals were frozen."

"Could you get up for a moment or two?"

"O, yes! I feel like a new man," answered the patient, who was not only strengthened but exhilarated by the strong liquor he had taken.

"Let me put these clothes on you."

"Clothes?" said the major, as he rose to his feet.

"Yes: I have a whole suit for you," replied Somers, as he assisted him to put on the dress he had brought.

They were warm and dry, and the poor fellow manifested a childish delight as he put them on. They were rather small, but they were warm and comfortable. To these was added the overcoat.

"Now, could you eat bacon and bread?" asked Somers.

"Could I eat them? I could if I had them."

"You have them," replied his attentive friend, as he brought the basket to his couch.

They both ate heartily, and when they had finished, De Banyan declared that he could walk ten miles more that night.

Somers knew that he could not — that he was under the influence of the brandy, and over-estimated his strength.

When he left the hospital he was as feeble as an infant, and nothing but the flashing hope of freedom could have sustained his weak body in the battle with the bloodhounds, and the walk from the creek. His friend determined to keep him quiet for a few days, if possible, assured that otherwise the enterprise must fail.

"Do you feel warm?" asked Somers, when he had told the story of his visit to the house.

"All but my feet," replied the patient.

"I will warm them," added the devoted nurse, as he took from his pocket a pair of socks, which he had transferred from the old to the new suit. "These are my fighting socks, but they shall do the best work now they have ever done."

De Banyan protested, but Somers persisted, and put the cherished mementoes of Lilian upon his feet.

"Now go to sleep," continued Somers, as he adjusted the overcoat, and placed the rags — of which the major had divested himself — on his feet.

He went to sleep, and Somers departed on an exploring expedition. In a pine forest, half a mile distant, he found an old shanty, which had been used for men engaged in drawing pitch from the trees. To this he transferred his patient, and kept him there for a week. The negroes on the plantation discovered the fugitives, but they were faithful friends, and supplied them with food and bed-clothes, so that they were quite comfortable.

From these devoted allies of the Union army, Somers learned that the deceased person he had seen in the house was the son of the planter, who had been sent home wounded. The articles taken had been missed, but the robbery was attributed to a couple of negroes who had run away at the time.

De Banyan gained strength each day, now that he was well clothed and well fed. After a week's rest, the fugitives started again, guided by a negro belonging to the plantation, who conducted them to the river, and provided them with a boat. Night after night they floated down the stream, guided and fed by the negroes, till they reached the sea, and went on board of one of the blockaders.

Once more they were beneath the old flag; once more they were in the hands of friends; and from their hearts went up the song of jubilee to Him who had guided and strengthened them in their pilgrimage from darkness and death to light and liberty. When they reached Port Royal, they heard of the capture of Savannah and the conquering march of Sherman from Atlanta to the sea. Then they sang a new song of jubilee, for the days of the rebellion were numbered.

## CHAPTER XXX.

### MAJOR SOMERS AND FRIENDS.

SOMERS and De Banyan proceeded from Port Royal to Washington, by the way of Fortress Monroe. "Fighting Joe" was no longer in the field of active operations, and our officers resigned their positions on the staff. The doughty general had won the admiration of the nation; the present generation will gratefully remember his efficient services, and posterity will enroll his name among the ablest and bravest defenders of the Union.

The term of service of the major's regiment had expired, and it had been sent home, and mustered out. Consequently he was out of employment. Somers was determined that he should not remain so long. There was a certain Senator Guilford in Washington, who considered himself under strong obligations to the young officer, and Somers immediately paid his respects to the distinguished man. He was warmly greeted, and when he had told his story, he was bold enough to ask a great favor for his friend.

"I will do what I can for him, Captain Somers, you may be sure. I remember him well, and I have always heard excellent accounts of him from your friend the general."

"There is not a better man in the service, sir; and he is worthy of any place which the government can give him," replied Somers, warmly.

"I know he is. By the way, captain, a certain general called upon me in relation to your affairs more than a year ago."

"Indeed, sir?" And Somers understood that he was indebted to the senator for his position in the regular army. "I am very grateful to you, Mr. Guilford."

"Don't mention it; my daughter, whose life you saved, thinks I have not half paid the debt yet."

"You have more than paid it, sir; and if I had known that I was indebted to you for my position, I should hardly have dared to speak to you in behalf of Major de Banyan."

"Don't be modest, Captain Somers. I have no scruples whatever in asking favors for such officers as yourself and your friend. I invariably refuse to say a word for any military man, unless I know that he is thoroughly meritorious. But, captain, you do not ask for my daughter."

"I heard she was married, and lived in Philadelphia," replied Somers, with some confusion.

"That is the case; she often speaks of you, and when you pass through Philadelphia you must see her."

"I will certainly do so, sir," replied the captain, as he took his leave.

Three days after he received a note from the senator, with De Banyan's commission as a major in the regular army. He hastened to communicate the news to his friend. The gratitude of the major knew no bounds, and he declared that Somers had been more to him than all the rest of the world. A furlough of thirty days had been granted them, and they started, the one for Pinchbrook, and the other for Tennessee, in search of his son, who had returned to Nashville when the army moved from Chattanooga.

On the way home Somers called upon the senator's daughter, and found her as pleasing, as pretty, and as grateful as ever; but his heart was farther north, and he hastened to the waiting arms of his loving friends. Lilian wept with joy when she saw him, and grandmother Ashford insisted upon telling about the defence of Boston during the "last war."

"Lilian, I have lost my socks," said Somers, when Mrs. Ashford had safely returned to their homes the firemen who went out to cut away the bridges in case of an invasion. "I had to put them on my friend De Banyan's feet, when he had nearly perished from cold and exhaustion."

"I am so glad you did!"

"I suffered myself, in Andersonville and Columbia, rather than wear them out, but I could not resist the appeal of my suffering friend."

"I am glad you did not."

"De Banyan is a noble fellow," added Somers.

"Shall I never see him?"

"I hope you will;" and she did, as the reader will soon learn.

Somers went to Pinchbrook, and was welcomed as one who had come forth from the grave. His mother wept over him, his father rejoiced over him, and Captain Barney, the friend of the family, "crowed" over him. He spent his thirty days between Boston and Pinchbrook, and at the end of that time reported for duty in Washington. He was ordered to join the regiment in which he had been commisioned, then in the line before Petersburg. In the bloody battle for the recovery of Fort Steadman, which had been captured by the rebels in a night attack, he was one of the first to mount the rampart, and turn the tide against the enemy. He fought with desperation, and urged his men to deeds of valor, which did much to retrieve the fortunes of the day.

For his heroic conduct on that eventful morning, he was made a major. De Banyan was there also, and what one did for his company the other did for his regiment. The brave Tennesseean was not forgotten nor

27*

overlooked. His merit was promptly recognized, and when the conquering host moved forward in pursuit of the flying brigades of the rebels, he was a brigadier general of volunteers.

Then came to them in the field, and then flashed over the telegraph wires to all parts of the nation, the thrilling intelligence that Richmond was captured. Still the indomitable Grant drew his gripe tighter and tighter upon the scattering hordes of the Rebellion; still Meade pressed on, and still Sheridan thundered over and through the shattered host of treason, until Lee surrendered the remnant of the vaunted army of Northern Virginia. The gallant Army of the Potomac was there to witness the humiliation of its old enemy.

All over the land cannon roared, bells pealed, bonfires blazed, and all the people shouted "Glory, Hallelujah," as the military power of the Rebellion crumbled and fell. Firmly had it stood, defying freedom, justice, and humanity; it drooped and expired almost in the twinkling of an eye.

The nation was filled with joy. Soldiers, sailors, and civilians rejoiced together, and from the hearts of all rose the pæan of thanksgiving for the victory which had crowned our arms. Then, in the midst of the people's gladness, came the terrible shock of the assassination of the nation's ruler — of the wise, noble, and good President Lincoln; and the redeemed Union was shrouded in mourning for him, who fell just as he rose to the glory of the mighty work he had accomplished.

The war was virtually ended. The surrender of Lee was followed by that of Johnston, and others in command of portions of the rebel army. The regiment to which Major Somers belonged was ordered to garrison a post; and De Banyan, who was attached to the same regiment, but for brave and skilful conduct in one of Sheridan's mighty charges, had been promoted to the rank of lieutenant colonel, also joined the command when his brigade was dissolved.

"General De Banyan, we meet again!" exclaimed Somers, as they joined hands, after several months of separation.

"Glory, Hallelujah!" shouted the general. "The war is over! The Union is saved! Rebellion is forever crushed! Somers, my dear fellow, I would hug you if it were dignified for a lieutenant colonel to do such a thing."

"Never mind your dignity, general. I feel like being silly, now that 'this cruel war is over.' I am delighted to see you. Do you remember Columbia? Do you remember the blood-hounds?"

"Shall I ever forget them?" replied De Banyan, feelingly.

"Do you remember that night when we reached the Augusta road?"

"I could not forget that any more than I could forget you," answered the general, as he again wrung the hand of his devoted friend. "Somers, our country is saved. We have fought it through to the end."

"We have had a hard time of it. Do you suppose, De Banyan, if it were to be done over again, you would be willing to go through with it once more?" asked Somers.

"Upon my soul, I should!" replied the general, warmly. "If I knew I had to die on the cold, wet ground, by the side of the Augusta road, after three years of hard service, I would go in as cheerfully as I would eat my dinner when I am hungry. Somers, if there is any man that loves his country, I do. I am willing to fight for her, and willing to die for her. This was a most infernal rebellion, and I thank God I have lived to see the end of it."

"So do I," responded Somers, fervently.

With the end of the war ends our story, though a few months later, an interesting event occurred in Boston, which we have not the heart to withhold from our readers, who have patiently followed our hero through his career of duty and suffering. As they have seen him in the carnage of battle, in the toils of the foe, in the loathsome prison camps of the rebels, so should they now see him in the hour of his greatest earthly joy. The event to which we allude was chronicled in the papers of the city as follows: —

"December 7, by the Rev. Dr. ———, Major Thomas Somers, of the ———th United States Infantry, to Miss Lilian Ashford, daughter of Richard C. Ashford, Esq., of this city. (No Cards.)"

No. — Rutland Street was brilliantly illuminated, as the stars broke forth from the storm clouds of that snowy Thanksgiving evening. There was a select assemblage of gentlemen, civil and military, and of ladies, young and old, from the matrons in sober black, to the maidens decked in colors appropriate to the joyous occasion. "Fighting Joe" had been cordially invited, but a severe illness alone prevented his attendance.

Half an hour before the time appointed for the ceremony, a carriage stopped at the door, from which stepped a tall gentleman, dressed in an elegant new uniform, on the shoulder-straps of which glistened the silver leaves that indicated his rank. With nervous energy he dashed up the steps, and endangered the bell wire by the desperate pull he gave. His summons was promptly answered by a colored gentleman in white cotton gloves.

"Major Somers," said the gentleman, sententiously.

"The major is engaged just now, sir, and cannot be seen," replied the waiter.

"Can't be seen!" exclaimed the arrival.

"Not just now, sir. Walk in, if you please, sir."

"Tell him Colonel De Banyan is here; and if that don't fetch him, say 'Magenta' to him."

The waiter went up stairs to the front room, where the bride and groom and their more intimate friends were assembled.

"Colonel De Banyan, from Magenta, sir, is —"

"From where?" roared Somers, jumping from his chair, so thoroughly convulsed with laughter that the buttons on his new coat threatened to be wrenched from their proper spheres. "Show him up," added he, when he could speak the words.

"My dear Somers, I am with you once again," said the colonel, as he rushed into the room and seized his friend by both hands. "From the deepest depths of an honest heart I congratulate you upon your approaching happiness."

"Thank you, general. I am delighted to see you," replied Somers. "It needed only your presence to complete my happiness."

"Mrs. Somers, I greet you," continued the colonel, dashing towards the old lady, and saluting her with the most courtly elegance.

"Sakes alive!" exclaimed the happy matron. "If it ain't Captain de Bangyang."

"Colonel de Banyan, if you please, is my present appellation; though I am sometimes called General de Banyan. I trust you are quite well, madam."

"Well, I'm pretty toler'ble, I thank ye, General de Bang— Well, I'm — I declare, I'm so flustrated I can't speak a word to-night."

"Madam, you are the proud and happy mother of the noblest young man in this noble republic," said the colonel, magnificently.

"Excuse me, De Banyan, but there is a lady here who has long desired to make your acquaintance," interposed Somers, as he led his friend to another part of the room, where Lilian sat, blushing and beautiful.

"Lilian, this is my friend, General de Banyan. General, Miss Ashford."

"Miss Ashford," said the general, with a dignified bow, as he took the gloved hand that was extended to him, "I bend in homage before one who is mighty enough in her beauty and her virtues to win the heart of my friend Major Somers."

Lilian blushed deeper than ever as she expressed her pleasure at meeting the man who had shared the toils and the sufferings of her intended husband.

"Miss Ashford, I have long known you, though we now meet for the first time; but permit me to add, that my friend is the only man in the United States who is worthy of the hand which is so soon to be his," added De Banyan, who was clearly in a "magnificent" mood on this occasion.

"I am afraid I shall be jealous of you, general," laughed Lilian.

"Nay, the major's heart is big enough to hold us all,

Miss Ashford," continued De Banyan, still holding the little hand. "I pray to God that he may never be called upon to do as much for you as he has done for me. When you sink down to die upon the cold, wet ground in winter, exhausted by sickness, borne under by starvation, with the savage blood-hounds baying in the distance, and more savage rebels lying in wait for you; when you lie down to die under these awful conditions, and he" — pointing to the major — " steps between you and the quaking messenger of death, who already has a gripe upon you; when he, at the imminent peril of his life, procures food and clothing to restore you; when he has stood over you like an angel, and won back the breath of life to your feeble body; when he has done this for you, you will know him as I know him."

As he finished, a great tear slid down each side of his bronzed face; but he dashed it away, and smiled again. Lilian pressed the great hand she held, and a tear burned among the roses of her bright cheek.

"But all this, and more, has he done for me!" exclaimed Somers, pointing to the colonel. "When I was wounded and helpless — "

"Upon my word, we are getting sentimental, major; and we had better subside," interposed the colonel. "Introduce me to the rest of the people."

Somers complied; and to each De Banyan made one

of his characteristic speeches; and perhaps he would have been voted ridiculous, if his eloquence had not a moment before started the tears of more than half the persons in the room.

Among those present was John Somers, the major's twin brother, who had come home to participate in this festive scene. On his arm was a beautiful young lady; but who and what she was, we must, for prudential reasons, decline to explain in this volume.

The clergyman came; the ceremony was performed, and the interesting incidents which follow it were duly and properly disposed of; and never was a happy couple more sincerely congratulated.

"Mrs. Somers, permit me to express my warmest hopes for your future happiness," said De Banyan. "May your husband be to you all that he has been to me; he can be no more; he will be no less."

There was nothing to mar the harmony of the occasion. Grandmother Ashford mercifully permitted the heroes of the "last war" to rest in their honored graves; and all gave a hearty God-speed to the happy couple, as they twain set out on the blissful journey of wedlock.

Major Somers is a man of good motives, and of high Christian principles, won in the day of trial and suffering, no less than in prosperity; and we doubt not he will be as true to his God, his country, and himself, in the future, as he has been in the past; when, by his fidelity, his bravery, and his patriotism, he carved out his fortunes on the battle-fields of The Great Rebellion.

www.ingramcontent.com/pod-product-compliance
Lightning Source LLC
Chambersburg PA
CBHW021155230426
43667CB00006B/407